Praise for *The Warrior Within*

"Warriors, as Air Force veteran D.J. Vanas shows us, are not the square-jawed, broad-shouldered, two-dimensional characters we so often watch on the screen. They aren't fearless, are rarely brilliant, and lose as often as they win. But in his thoughtful *The Warrior Within*, Vanas captures the essence of steadfast courage, self-discipline, and resilience that describes those among us who embody the true warrior spirit."

—General Stanley McChrystal (U.S. Army, ret.),
author of *Risk* and *Team of Teams*

"The powerful lessons imparted in these chapters will inspire strength, confidence, and motivation, so that you can deliver your best in the worst of circumstances—while keeping your sanity and health! I encourage every healthcare giver to read *The Warrior Within*, for they truly serve, fight, protect and heal every day, often at their own expense." —LeAnn Thieman, author of the Chicken Soup for Nurse's Soul series and founder of SelfCare for HealthCare

"I highly recommend *The Warrior Within*! Through great storytelling, D.J. Vanas shares an often overlooked element of leadership: taking care of yourself. Our beautiful Anishinaabe teachings emphasize balance in all things. Being a warrior means recognizing your needs and honoring your gifts. Way to go, D.J.!"

—Angeline Boulley (Sault Ste. Marie Tribe of Chippewa Indians),
New York Times bestselling author of *Firekeeper's Daughter*

"D.J. Vanas inspires us to find our 'warrior spirit' of courage, perseverance, resilience, and teamwork in life's most fearful times. Your heart will soar like an eagle as you read how ordinary heroes use this inner strength to serve others—and how we can learn to do the same."

—Assistant Chief Joseph Pfeifer (FDNY, ret.), author of *Ordinary Heroes*

"This is it: the book I've been waiting for! There isn't another on the market that applies indigenous principles and ideas in order to expose the warrior in you. A comprehensive, compelling, emotional and amazingly insightful book. I couldn't put it down. I wish I had this book years ago!"   —Juanita Mullen (Seneca), AI/AN veterans liaison, Department of Veterans Affairs

"D.J. Vanas describes a life of leading and doing through Indigenous identity and values. Combining his personal story with advice, *The Warrior Within* is more than a leadership book. It is a story of living a life of abundance and rich relationships, with D.J. as your terrific guide."

—Cheryl Crazy Bull, president and CEO, American Indian College Fund

"*The Warrior Within* is more than a book; it's a leadership tool written by a man who emulates its teachings in his personal and professional lives. Packed full of real-world anecdotes and practical advice on facing adversity and dealing with change, it will empower you to face life's battles with honor and courage. Embrace its teachings and you will certainly cultivate your warrior within!"

—Lieutenant Colonel Waldo Waldman (U.S. Air Force, ret.), executive coach and author of *Never Fly Solo*

"D.J. has captured the essence of being a warrior in a thoughtful, deeply meaningful way. No matter how successful we may be professionally, personally, or financially, we all struggle with challenges along the way. Recognizing your fallibility doesn't make you less capable; rather, it adds to the strength of your experience. D.J. helps us view the warrior spirit as a journey, rather than a destination."

—Commander John B. Herrington (U.S. Navy, ret.), first Native American astronaut

"This book is for readers who want to tap into something deeper—that warrior spirit Vanas so eloquently describes—to serve at their best every day, and become strong enough to do it for a lifetime. Filled with the distilled wisdom of the ages and proven in the toughest of times, Vanas shows you how to become more tenacious, courageous, and, ultimately, a warrior of good. A fantastic read! If understanding and applying the warrior spirit were an Olympic sport, D.J. Vanas would win the gold medal!"   —Ruben Gonzalez, four-time Olympian and author of *The Courage to Succeed*

The
Warrior
Within

The
Warrior
Within

OWN YOUR POWER TO SERVE, FIGHT, PROTECT, AND HEAL

D.J. Vanas

PORTFOLIO | PENGUIN

Portfolio / Penguin
An imprint of Penguin Random House LLC
penguinrandomhouse.com

Most Portfolio books are available at a discount when purchased in
quantity for sales promotions or corporate use. Special editions, which
include personalized covers, excerpts, and corporate imprints, can be created
when purchased in large quantities. For more information, please call (212)
572-2232 or email specialmarkets@penguinrandomhouse.com. Your local
bookstore can also assist with discounted bulk purchases using the Penguin
Random House corporate Business-to-Business program. For assistance in
locating a participating retailer, email B2B@penguinrandomhouse.com.

ISBN 9780593423011 (hardcover)
ISBN 9780593423028 (ebook)

Printed in the United States of America
1st Printing

Book design by Alexis Farabaugh

This book is dedicated to the Creator
who continues to guide and strengthen me . . .

‑!‑

And to my luminescent, effervescent daughters,
Gabrielle and Isabella, who bring so much joy, light, and love
into my world. Even in the storms, you both keep finding ways
to move forward. You inspire me and you're both warriors
in the making. I'm blessed beyond words to be your dad and
proud of each of you for a million reasons, but most of
all because you both have such good hearts . . . and aren't
afraid to use them. I love you both with all of mine.

Contents

INTRODUCTION

Bent over, exhausted, shaking, and bleeding from my chest, I watched the crimson droplets make puffs of dust where they landed. The sweet, pungent smells of burning medicines like sage, sweetgrass, and cedar wafted all around. My mouth was as dry as a kiln and my head throbbed, but my heart soared with the high pitch of eagle bone whistles blowing all around me.

I had just finished my final year of the Sun Dance, a traditional tribal ceremony of gratitude that takes place over four years. We dance for four days each summer, from sunup to sundown without food or water, to pray for thanksgiving, to offer thanks for our blessings, and to ask the spirit that brought the pipe to guide us in prayer and connect us to the Creator. On the third day, we pierce our chests with buffalo bone or wood skewers that are tied to ropes connected to the Tree of Life, which stands in the center of the ceremonial circle. We dance to the tree and back, to the literal end of our rope, four times. On the last journey we pull backward until we break free. As the mothers of the world push, push to bring children into the world, we men pull, pull to balance it out. It sounds like muffled firecrackers when the piercing sticks finally rip out of our skin and fly away.

Once the ceremony was over, my spiritual leader, Selo Black Crow (Oglala Lakota), grabbed me by my sage bracelet and looked into my tear-filled eyes. "Remember," he whispered, "you're a warrior now."

What I'd learned in that ceremony shattered the idea I'd had about the definition of a warrior up to that point. I grew up thinking that a warrior was a bright, shiny, iconic figure who was always brave, always strong, needed no help or encouragement from anyone, and always did the right thing and always had the right answers. Warriors didn't cry, screw up, stumble, or experience fear or pain. This was a person who was beyond needing anything but the next worthy challenge.

This, of course, was all bullshit.

When I was a kid, I was insecure and pudgy, wore off-brand clothes and thick plastic-rimmed glasses, and sported a bowl haircut parted down the middle. I felt out of place everywhere I went, though I was eager to please. Every one of my progress reports in middle school labeled me as "talking too much in class." I wanted people to like me, but felt ugly and weak and was scared much of the time. And I was trying to find my way in one of the roughest middle schools around. My look and demeanor made me a target for insults and bullying. Across the street from the largest public projects complex in southern Mississippi, I'd see people sitting on top of abandoned cars drinking 40s of malt liquor on my morning bus ride. It was common to see ambulances or police cars show up across the street during the school day. We had violence, drugs, teen pregnancies; we saw our principal get beat up when he tried to break up one of the frequent fights. But it wasn't so much fear that I felt during that period of my life, though there were many of those moments. I felt the raw vulnerability, helplessness, and insecurity of feeling weak and less than. I thought being a warrior meant I'd never have to feel those things. I wanted to feel strong. I wanted to be brave.

I grew up as a military brat and away from my tribe, the Ottawa Tribe (or Anishinaabe). Though I did know about my cultural heritage and our warrior tradition—and was proud of that—it didn't connect with me as a source of strength or something I could leverage at that point in my life. Out of frustration, I started pushing through the criticism, teasing, and insecurity of feeling like an outsider or the lonely nerd. I started to fight back in my mind, applying my skills in the classroom. I found confidence through achievement and following my own path. I wanted to go to college, and go on scholarship, so I started doubling down on academics. I got involved in athletics. I wanted to develop something in me that made me feel proud of myself. Special. Empowered. I was exercising the traits of a fighter, doing things that would benefit only me for now. But this was not the warrior path. Not yet.

My path led me to an appointment to the United States Air Force Academy, and four years later I graduated with a BS in management and the rank of second lieutenant in the Air Force. The military has a great service model and warrior concept, but something still felt off. Out of reach. The marketing for the military promoted a glossy image of heroic perfection that I felt I needed to live up to. To me, the role felt too big to fulfill and never quite seemed to fit, like wearing an oversize coat. It made the role seem unattainable. Impervious to pain. Always righteous and flawless. Never show weakness. The gap between how I saw that role and how I felt I was fulfilling it was exhausting at times because it didn't feel authentic. I sometimes felt like an impostor and out of alignment. (The military is working hard on changing the misconception of the "impervious warrior" due to high suicide rates from military members. The aversion to the stigma of seeking help leaves many service members wracked with depression, untreated PTSD, etc., and going without help until they are in crisis.)

I brought this conceptual struggle into my journey of the Sun Dance ceremony. What I learned through that experience, and since, has dismantled that fixed role and transformed it into something real, practical, and accessible. The warrior archetype I found finally "clicked" at a spiritual level. Learning from elders and tradition for decades, going through ceremony, having countless conversations with those living the principles, from single moms to social workers to business leaders to combat veterans, I finally found my truth and strength behind real warrior spirit.

Warriors are courageous, but it doesn't mean they aren't scared. Warriors are strong but also deal with doubts and heartbreak and cry at times in frustration. Warriors do fight for something bigger than self, but they don't neglect themselves or feel they must do it alone. Warriors lead by example but not perfect example. Warriors are protectors *and* peacekeepers. Warriors live their values, like courage and humility, but it doesn't mean they don't make mistakes. Overall, warriors endure and keep going even when they face tough odds, setbacks, or defeats, get the emotional shit kicked out of them, or start to lose heart. They do not quit. Rather, they find a way forward because they know, in the end, that it's not about them. It's who they serve and how they serve that really matter. It is a role based on these principles, and rooted in service, that transcends race, age, and gender. It is available and accessible for anyone willing to walk the path. That includes you.

Why Did I Write This Book?

We all want to be brave. We all want to be able to deliver when it matters. I know that feeling. I know what it's like to have great expectations from others, high responsibility, and pressure to perform—and at the same time face mouth-drying anxiety, confusion, and fear. We so want to deliver but sometimes neglect the mindsets and actions that allow us to do so.

I wrote this book to share one of the most compelling examples of strength and service I've ever encountered. For over twenty-five years I've been serving groups that are dedicated to serving others—from tribal employees to the Mayo Clinic and from teachers to NASA—and I've frequently noticed a disturbing situation: a misalignment that springs from having noble intentions but a hot mess in the execution. For all this time, I've seen people with big hearts and a willingness to serve get muddled up, become overwhelmed, lose confidence and clarity, and start edging closer and closer to burnout. Ultimately this dynamic creates the biggest threat to delivering great service to others: apathy.

I wrote this book to strengthen these warriors so they can deliver on the commitments they made to serve others well.

What is old is new again—and needed. We live in such a fast-paced and hyperconnected world, where information overload is normal. Our tribal traditions and Native concepts speak to these areas, offering a treasure trove of wisdom on how to find clarity and navigate a busy world, create better life balance, make real connection, stay strong and resilient, and leave a legacy of good in the process. These ways have always been around, but I'd argue they're needed now more than ever.

The warrior role in our tribal communities is a fascinating and powerful archetype, worthy of emulating on our journey today. It is built on the foundation of service, strength, and character. It encourages us to understand and use our abilities, to maintain clarity on our path, to bounce back from adversity, to surround ourselves with strength so we can be strong in our roles. I want to share these ideas not just with the hardworking service providers in the world at large, but within our tribal communities and especially our youth. Native people come from greatness, it's always been in us, and I want this book to be another reminder of why.

When you apply the ideas in this book to your own life, you'll have the power to transform your life and how you serve others. I've been using and sharing these ideas for twenty-five years. Not only have I seen firsthand positive impact in others when these concepts are used, but I have been a constant beneficiary of their power and promise.

As you go through the principles in this book, remember that change and growth are a process, not an event. I had to remind myself of that, even as I wrote this book, repeating, "I'm *writing* a book," not "I write a book." Not only would we sound like a bad Dick and Jane story, or a caveman, if we spoke like that, but it's also inaccurate. Remember, even small, stumbling steps in the right direction are still in the right direction! Be patient and encouraging with yourself and celebrate even the smallest victories. Sometimes we're rusty at this practice, or never learned to do it at all. If the latter is your case, then ask, "What would a supportive, encouraging person say to me in this moment?" and then act accordingly. Try it. You'll be pleasantly surprised when what you come up with can give you a spark of strength to keep going.

What This Book Is
(and What This Book Is Not)

This book is an explanation and practical application of common principles our Indigenous warriors followed with great success to fulfill and honor their roles. The lessons and stories I share in these pages come from personal experience, ceremonial traditions, and three decades of serving our Native communities and speaking with elders, veterans, and others engaged in service to their communities. I've attempted to capture the most relevant ideas that we can use to empower and transform our lives into something meaningful, exciting, and evergreen.

This is not a history or research book, a political treatise, or a message on behalf of Indian Country or my tribe. I do not speak for all Indigenous people either; nor is it my place to do so. I share these ideas independently, from my heart to yours. This book may be accused of perhaps being too general or even Pan-Indian in its approach, and that is a fair point. But it doesn't make the ideas less powerful or practical. It has been written that way consciously to stick with the common and useful principles we all can use.

One thing I've learned working in Indian Country for over twenty-five years is that the moment you start being too tribally specific is the moment that other tribal groups feel left out and that the ideas don't apply. We miss the point of the ideas and instead practice another way, unfortunately, to divide and conquer ourselves. I want to be as pragmatic as possible, keeping the ideas general but useful, for all of us. I also realize that not all tribes had a warrior tradition per se, some being more pacific and relational when dealing with conflict, but they still expressed a warrior spirit in those moments. These tribal leaders acted courageously despite the odds and served their people to the best of their abilities.

The history of Native Americans in this country is brutal and ugly and continues to be challenging. Government policies—including organized genocide, broken treaties, land theft, population removal, boarding schools, tribal termination, and much more—were designed and implemented to eliminate Native people, and our culture, and break our will. They failed but left damage that continues to affect us to this day. There are many great books that address these important topics, but this is not one of them. This book is meant to highlight the contribution of principles that our warriors showed, despite unbelievable odds, that have echoed throughout history and reverberate even now. The principles our warriors displayed were held in high esteem during their time (lauded and admired even by notables that did no favors for Native Americans, such as Kit Carson, George Washington, and even General George Custer, the bitterest of enemies) and have practical application today.

‑‑

To focus only on the tools that were used by Native American warriors of the past, the bow and arrow, tomahawk, or war club, is to lose the forest for the trees. My people, the Ottawa Tribe of Michigan, were warriors, and it was the mindset they had and how they practiced it that allowed them to do the amazing things they did. I think about the sacrifices they went through to allow me to be here today, what they endured on my behalf. They survived against incredible odds, despite being vastly outnumbered, outgunned, overmatched in technology, deceived at every turn, purposefully infected with diseases, starved out, and hunted—but they were never outmatched in warrior spirit. Our warrior spirit never died, which is one of the reasons why our Native American community consistently has the highest rates of military service of any ethnic group in America.

But the warrior spirit is also alive and well in every tribal community to which I travel. It's alive in those fighting to preserve our culture and language, the single parents or grandparents raising strong kids, those building safer and caring communities, or promoting education, healthcare, and economic opportunities. Still outnumbered and despite the odds, they're fulfilling the warrior role today.

The warrior model works because it has endured for millennia through some of the hardest times any group of people has ever known. I'm proud to be descended from warriors; our men were warriors, our women were warriors, and when they were eliminated, our children became warriors—and they still are. We used to fight to preserve what we had; now the fight is to preserve who we are. That fight has evolved beyond the physical and is now fought through a variety of means including intellectual, social, legal, economic, educational, and more. I work with these warriors, serve with them, and I'm constantly inspired by them. What I intend to do is unpack the ideas and concepts that apply to our own lives and careers, especially in these difficult and uncertain times.

I'm grateful that you're joining me on this journey and look forward to being your guide, your scout, on occasion a jester, a friend, a coach, and most of all, a fellow warrior on the path.

So, yell your war cry (I'll explain what this is later, of course) and let's get started. Aho!

Own Your Warrior Spirit

Putting It to Work

One morning, while I was still in the Air Force, I woke up with what I thought was the beginning of a heat rash running from the right side of my torso to the top of my thigh. Immediately after waking up, the bumps and tracks started burning like they'd been touched by a match. It felt like liquid fire under my skin. It was excruciating, and I wouldn't have wished this on my worst enemy. I had shingles, and it tormented me for six weeks of living hell.

During that time, I was an active-duty Air Force captain, serving as chief of minority enrollment at the U.S. Air Force Academy, my alma mater, where I led a full-time team of ten junior officers and advised a field team of another hundred. At the same time, we were just starting a family, and to complicate matters, I was also in the process of launching a new speaking and consulting business. I was committed to making a difference in the world by both serving with distinction in my military role and creating a business to impact communities, organizations, and individual lives in a positive, meaningful way.

In other words, I wanted to do it all, and I sure tried. I would get up at four in the morning to work on the business for three hours before going in to work. Then I would lead my team during the day, come home at five, and continue to work on the business until ten or eleven at night. I even worked on the business through the weekends, creating content, fine-tuning my programs, and building a database of contacts. But I felt the constant pulling tear of going in several directions at once, the overwhelming feeling of having too much on my plate, and the agonizing frustration of trying so hard to do my best for those I was responsible for serving. It was slowly breaking me down.

The more frustrated I got, the harder I worked, but the more I neglected myself, the more depleted I became. Eventually, I developed every classic sign of stress—headaches, upset stomach, restlessness, agitation, lack of focus. I was drinking Maalox and Pepto Bismol like they were protein shakes, eating Tums and Rolaids like candy, and kept saying, "I'll take care of myself later." I so desperately wanted to make an impact, to make a positive difference—and it was killing me.

Later showed up with a vengeance, and I suffered greatly

for it. I was twenty-eight at the time, and the doctor I saw explained that shingles, the resurgence of chicken pox due to stress, was usually something we get when we're older and our immunity isn't as strong. He asked me point-blank, "What are you doing to yourself?"

My intentions to serve were good, but my execution had become a mess. Through that experience, I learned a hard truth: *We can't be warriors when we're falling apart.*

-ʻ-

If you have a job that others depend on, and you serve in roles where your efforts have real-world impact and your best is required every day, even when you're not "feeling it"—this book is for you. Whether you're a frontline healthcare worker, a teacher advocating for education reform, an engineer coming up with new ways to insulate our cities from the effects of climate change, a deployed military member protecting our country, a dedicated government employee, a leader of a business team, or a social worker trying to help families stay together—if you're fighting to make a positive impact, you can do it consistently only when you own your own need to get yourself right.

I've met thousands of rising, established, and retired stars in healthcare, government, education, social work, and other service industries, and I've found that, almost without exception, everyone has experienced the painful, and sometimes dangerous, effects of having our intentions and execution out of alignment. The intention to serve was there, but they ultimately couldn't deliver because they weren't taking care of themselves in the process. Many of those I interviewed mentioned experiencing the battle damage of unaddressed health and wellness needs, from relationship and sleep problems to migraines, to becoming overweight due to stress eating, to experiencing a terrifying wave of ministrokes as a result of pushing beyond what they could bear.

When there is a strong will and intention to serve, there must also be an equally strong will and intention to serve the *right* way. This means honoring and following a set of principles that will keep you resilient, healthy, energized, and able to sustain the good fight. Without it, you suffer and fall short. Instead of being an asset and contributor to your tribe, you become a detriment to it. We can't respond to threats, leverage opportunities, serve others well, or navigate crises if we're already in a crisis ourselves.

Learning this lesson for myself inspired me to create the model that I'm sharing with you in this book. I looked to the past and found beautiful principles and a time-tested framework of perseverance and resilience through chaos followed by our warriors in tribal communities that enabled them to endure against incredible odds and unbelievable obstacles and remain resilient and effective. I found solutions to keep us strong in the fight, stay balanced, serve at our best through chaos, keep improving, and enjoy our lives of service so much more through the process. It's worked wonders for me and resonated deeply with thousands of service providers when they understand that the role of warriors can make us warriors in our roles. It can work for you too. These principles require no special background, affiliation, or training and are available for anyone choosing to use and benefit from them. And they are needed.

Before we learn how to become warriors in our roles, we must first learn what a warrior is. And that begins with breaking down what a warrior is not.

What a Warrior Is Not

The word "warrior" is loaded with emotion and comes with a host of dangerous expectations, behaviors, and stereotypes. Throughout history, our Native American warriors have been constantly misrepresented, typically seen only through the lens of their fighting skills. In the media, Hollywood in particular, a warrior is often portrayed as a chiseled, fearless, and violent character who destroys scores of enemies and city blocks, who shoots eight million bullets, bazookas, bad guys, and surly looks at the camera, all in the name of glory.

These stereotypical media images not only foster toxic personas bent on dominating others, but they also create harmful and unrealistic expectations of perfection and invulnerability. Living out those harmful expectations leaves committed servants under tremendous pressure to not make mistakes, not ask for help—or even admit that they need it. This leaves those same people suffering in silence or working so hard they're burned out beyond repair, harming their health and relationships, and actually doing more damage than good.

A WARRIOR ISN'T JUST A MAN'S JOB

Women are the birthplace and backbone of our tribal nations. They've always had a strong presence, serving as chiefs in matriarchal tribes, but rose to a special place of prominence after the Great Indian Wars. Many of our men were either killed or spiritually broken, having been disarmed and forced to farm, as hunting, our cultural and spiritual way of life, was greatly restricted or forbidden by the U.S. government and its institutions. Our women became full-fledged warriors in every sense of the word as they protected children, kept families intact, and fought to preserve our culture. They've been honorably fulfilling that role for almost 150 years and undoubtedly will continue to do so, not only in our tribal communities but also in government and military service, education, science, social services, healthcare, and leadership roles across industries.

Society in general continues to change, becoming more equitable and erasing stereotypical roles that locked women into fixed responsibilities and behaviors. As the proud father of two amazing daughters, I'm thrilled to see this change continue to progress. Warriors in our communities include Autumn Peltier (Anishinaabe/Wikwemikong First Nation in Canada), who was nominated for the International Children's Peace Prize at the age of thirteen and told the UN to "warrior up" in protecting clean drinking water for future generations. Wilma

Mankiller (Cherokee) had her tires slashed and endured death threats to become the first woman elected to serve as principal chief of the Cherokee Nation. U.S. Army soldier Lori Ann Piestewa (Hopi) was the first Native American woman killed in combat on foreign soil during the war in Iraq.

There are countless warriors who don't fit into the warrior stereotype yet are making a positive impact in the world. This is a welcome evolution of the role, blunting the toxic masculinity that may have blighted this role in the past, making it inaccessible or unapproachable to our mighty women. The *modern* traditional warrior role would be incomplete without them.

A WARRIOR ISN'T IN IT FOR THE GLORY

Think of all the work you do in your role. Let's be honest here. Most of what you do, you don't get credit for, right? But you do it anyway because you know it's the right thing to do and you've committed to doing it to the best of your ability. When we make a mistake, it seems we get called on it from every direction. But doing a great job in your role may feel like wetting your pants in a dark suit—it makes you feel warm and tingly but no one else really notices. That is tough, but when we know we're in it not for the glory but for the impact, it makes this reality much easier to navigate.

A WARRIOR DOESN'T GO AT IT ALONE

What can you do with a single finger? Poke an eye, pick your nose, or give someone "the finger." But you can't manipulate a doorknob, open a pickle jar, or hold someone's hand. You need your other fingers to do that. Going at it solo not only limits our ability to create impact but can also quickly lead us to what I call "overwhelm" and burnout. Our warriors understood the power of a tribe and never fought alone for that reason.

A WARRIOR ISN'T ARROGANT

When you're active, busy, and starting to get results, it is easy to drift into a mentality of dominance. Dominance can breed arrogance, where we place ourselves above all those who are fighting beside us to make a difference. If left unchecked, that arrogance can lead us to step on others to move ourselves forward or to get our way. Arrogance weakens our ability to collaborate with others and therefore our ability to serve effectively.

A WARRIOR ISN'T BULLETPROOF

We must avoid the temptation to overromanticize the role of the warrior as we so often do. When we do that, we sell their character and achievements short and keep the warrior role out of reach. Our legendary warriors like Tecumseh, Crazy

Horse, Osceola, and Chief Joseph are often cloaked in an aura of invincibility in which they needed no one and were impervious to hurts or doubts. But of course, they dealt with fear, faced pain, and stumbled. They needed outside resources, encouragement, and self-care, as do we all. They were human beings, not Hollywood superheroes.

What a Warrior Is

A WARRIOR IS DIFFERENT FROM A FIGHTER

A warrior needs to be a fighter, but there is a difference between being a fighter and a warrior. A fighter is someone who leverages their time, talent, and effort toward an objective, and the primary beneficiary is that individual. This is critically important in self-improvement and spurs us to go back to school, leave bad relationships, get a better job, stand up for ourselves, or lose weight. We need to be willing and able to fight for the things that improve our life or else they don't happen.

However, fighting for the self is not the role of a warrior. Warriors take those hard-earned lessons and skills and use them to serve others and impact their world in a positive way.

My friend Nancy Griffin (Saginaw Chippewa) is a powerful example of how a fighter can become a warrior. She grew up in an abusive home and married an abuser. She wanted to serve and fight for others as a rehabilitation counselor to help those with disabilities get employment, but she first had to fight for herself. She went back to school, but says, "I would go to classes after being beat up, which was usually around finals, with black eyes, broken nose, and broken bones. You get to a place where you think this is all life has to offer." But a committed passion to serve pulled her through her fear, doubt, and painful situation.

Through lots of support, encouragement, and a warrior spirit in action, Nancy started making different choices, including a divorce. She decided to change her circumstances by changing her choices. "A medicine man prayed for me and told me I had a future, though many times I couldn't see beyond the moment." Nancy fought step-by-step to change her situation, get her education, and become a warrior equipped, trained, and able to serve others. Because of her, several hundred people have become successfully employed over the expanse of her career. At one point, Nancy had the highest success rate in the state of Michigan for minority youth getting and maintaining employment!

A WARRIOR FIGHTS FOR SOMETHING BIGGER THAN THE SELF

My people (Ottawa) called a warrior *ogichidaa*, and that term has little to do with what we see in the media portrayal mentioned earlier. It's not about being the toughest person, it's not about seeking glory, and it doesn't require a uniform or combat boots. A warrior is fully engaged in developing their talent and ability over a lifetime to become an asset to the "tribe" they serve. Today, that tribe might be your family, community, company, students, patients, clients, or taxpaying citizens. But make no mistake, we all have one to serve.

A WARRIOR NURTURES THEIR WARRIOR SPIRIT

In our tribal communities, the warrior role was a spiritual endeavor as much as anything else. Between ceremonies, prayer, sacrifices, and use of holy medicines, spirit was interwoven throughout all their actions and intentions. When our spirit is involved in an activity, the activity itself becomes a spiritual event, and we're answering to a higher power and higher purpose. We're all in. When we incorporate our own spiritual beliefs and practices into our efforts, they can pull us through pain and fear and help us get out of our own way to accomplish what we set out to do.

Your warrior spirit is the driving force to face and overcome challenges and to develop yourself so you can serve and contribute to your tribe. It is a can-do, persistent, resilient, optimistic, uncompromising attitude composed of grit, determination, love for what is fought for, consistent focus, courageous commitment, and a willingness to own mistakes. Your warrior spirit is that voice inside you that shouts, "I will find a way forward!" and surpasses motivation.

In my experience, it is so often the missing piece in personal or professional success and serving others well. We can have all the resources in the world when it comes to budget, time, or personnel, but if the *warrior spirit* is missing, those resources won't translate into success. After all, the greatest obstacle to delivering great service to others is usually not a lack of resources anyway. The greatest obstacle is often apathy.

You may have encountered and leveraged your own warrior spirit when you overcame a challenge that scared the hell out of you, navigated a dramatic change, had to work harder than you thought possible, were painted into a corner, backed up against a wall, or in crisis. You dug deep in those moments and pulled out that "no-quit force" that we're going to explore in this book. These pages will show you how to strengthen your warrior spirit, put it to work, and use it more effectively—and at will.

A WARRIOR IS DRIVEN BY SERVICE

There are three reasons why service is at the heart of the warrior role:

First, service is our highest calling and most fulfilling endeavor—not just to tribal warriors but to us as warriors in our roles too. Think about the purpose of our being and our role within the human family. If we're not put here to be of service to others, why are we here at all? A warrior is clear in their purpose, which is to feed and protect their tribe, not their ego.

Second, service is our deepest need. *Everyone* has a need to feel valued, that our work matters, that we matter. You have it, I have it, our kids, clients, and teammates have it. And we can get some of that need fulfilled when we are *of service* to others. How wonderful is that?

Third, service is our legacy. It's what we leave behind us

when we're gone. I've served over five hundred tribal nations in the last twenty-five years, and when those tribal communities lose an elder, they have a feast in their memory where they reflect on that elder's life and what made them special. Guess what they talk about? Not the elder's nice clothes, the car they drove, or where they vacationed. They talk about who they helped, encouraged, or guided. They laugh about the stories that elder shared to brighten someone else's day and lift them out of the dark. They discuss the times that elder provided a shoulder to cry on or shared stories of hope, strength, or wisdom with those who needed them most. They talk about their legacy, the beautiful moments left behind that were born from serving others well.

In the same way, when we are gone from this world, the legacy we'll leave behind us lives on through the moments of connection, service, and impact we had in other people's lives. And we're creating that legacy each day of our journey.

A WARRIOR LEADS WITH LOVE ABOVE ALL ELSE

Let's talk about love. A fight *for* anything requires energy, focus, and time—all are valuable resources. So if you don't love what you're fighting for, then why the hell are you fighting for it? Why is it even on your radar? When we love what we're fighting for, as our warriors of the past did for their people, we are willing to make hard choices and are committed to seeing them through. Our heart is a powerful element in our warrior role and including it in our efforts is a game changer.

A WARRIOR MAY SURRENDER,
BUT THEY NEVER QUIT

Though our tribal warriors were not able to stem the tide of Manifest Destiny, technological advances, and endless waves of settlers and soldiers, one would be hard-pressed to lodge an argument that our warriors didn't fight and negotiate with maximum effort. In fact, many warriors, like Crazy Horse and Chief Joseph, would have fought until the bitter end but were thinking of the future of their people and tribe when they finally surrendered. This required the warrior principle of fighting for (and thinking of) something bigger than self. Our warriors may have surrendered, for the good of their people and the survival of the tribe, but they *never* quit!

When we quit, we just stop trying and putting forth the effort. We start talking ourselves out of the challenge, pointing out why it won't work, and finding selective proof that we're right in our assessment. "It's too hard," or, you might think, "I'm not sure." Fear or frustration starts to dominate. When we quit, we feel the sting of walking away from something that could've been a success. The danger with quitting is that the next time things get tough, it's much easier to quit the second time. It's a bad habit to foster.

Surrender is something else, and it occurs when we come to the end of our power. We realize we have no more leverage, our actions are no longer effective or having any impact, we can do no more to change or improve the situation, and maybe we see we're doing more harm than good. There's no shame in surrender, and in fact it can be one of the bravest things we do. Asking for help, finding another way, or letting something go that isn't working anymore—whether that's a job or a relationship—requires courage. When we make the distinction between quitting and surrender, we gain clarity and guidance as we fight through our challenges.

And let's be clear about the term "victory." Victory is not necessarily creating a spectacular outcome that is exactly what we intended. We don't necessarily control that dynamic. But victory can be defined by the amount and quality of dedicated effort we put forth—we *do* control that.

Some of the biggest victories I've ever had in my life happened in moments I could've defined as defeat, but knowing I put forth my best made it feel like a win and prepared me for the next challenge.

When I was a senior at the U.S. Air Force Academy, I took on a Don Quixote–like quest to train for a spot on our coveted USAFA boxing team in the Wing Open tournament. Everyone thought I was nuts. Senior year, our first-class year, was supposed to be enjoyed to the maximum (legal) level. This was a military academy, after all, and I devoted years there to high-tempo, grueling activities, rigid structure, and mind-scorching academics. Nevertheless, I trained my guts out for the boxing team, suffering painful shin splints, cutting twenty pounds down to my fight weight, and sometimes eating only an apple for dinner.

Then, two weeks before the tournament, I broke my nose for the second time, and this time, the crack went toward my eye orbital. This meant I was done. And I was devastated. I had a heart-to-heart with Coach Weichers and cried in his office. The legendary coach, not known for warm fuzzies, not only showed compassion that amazed me, but a few days later gave me a handwritten letter I carry to this day. In it, he praised my work ethic and dedication to a valiant attempt, though it may have fallen short of my own goal. For that reason, not making the team has never felt like a defeat.

_'_

Warriors served our tribal communities for millennia, and now their principles can be applied in our roles to get us better results in our ability to serve others today. Too many of us have misalignment of intention and execution, which so often leads to burnout.

At the end of the day, a true warrior doesn't do it for the glory, doesn't go it alone, isn't arrogant—and is definitely not bulletproof. A warrior fights for something bigger than self, nurtures their warrior spirit, incorporates love as a source of strength, and understands that service is at the heart of it all. Finally, under the right circumstances warriors may surrender, but they never quit.

After all, victory is in the effort, not necessarily the outcome. I was reminded of that working with the Special Olympics in Florida a few years ago. I was assisting a preteen boy named Trey during a surfing match. At least in my mind, I thought we were competing for points. He eagerly tried and would giggle with delight every time he caught a wave. He was eager and giggled even when he didn't catch a wave. His vision of victory was just to do his best in the activity, not to best anybody else. And if you don't know the motto for the Special Olympics, I'll share it here:

"Let me win. But if I cannot win, let me be brave in the attempt."

Now that is a motto worthy of a warrior . . .

2

Live Off
the Land

Using What You've Got Right Now

n 1972, LeAnn was a young pediatrics nurse when she bought a dozen cupcakes at a bake sale to help the Friends of Children of Viet Nam (FCVN) organization during the Vietnam War. Fast-forward to April 1975, and she was answering the first in a series of questions to a high-stakes problem: How do you smuggle $10,000 into Vietnam? Answer: Impersonate Dolly Parton.

LeAnn had enrolled as a volunteer for the FCVN and was about to go through customs with a comically overstuffed bra filled with cash because the Vietnamese dollar no longer had any value. She was on a mission to escort six Amerasian babies, called as such during that time because they had a Vietnamese mother and an American serviceman father, out of Vietnam for adoption in the United States. These children were targets of hatred—and retribution—by the North Vietnamese Army, who committed terrible acts of vengeance on them.

When LeAnn finally reached the orphanage where she would retrieve the babies, she was told that she wouldn't be taking six babies back to the United States—she would be taking three hundred! President Ford had just authorized Operation Babylift to rescue as many Amerasian orphans as possible. The handful of volunteers, both Vietnamese and Americans alike, began leveraging all their creativity, know-how, and available resources to make it happen.

The day of the exodus was a steamy 106 degrees. LeAnn and the volunteer team had a city bus available, but it couldn't reach the orphanage, which was located at the end of a narrow dirt road, so they had to create a makeshift transport shuttle to reach the bus—and they had to do it fast. Bombs and artillery shells were already striking the outskirts of the city, rattling windows and walls.

How do you get twenty-two babies at a time up a dirt road to a city bus? Answer: Grab a VW van, take the center seats out, and lay all the babies on the floor like cookies on a baking sheet.

Once they got a first load of fifty babies on the city bus, the volunteers placed two or three babies per seat—but there were no seat belts or baby seats. To keep the babies from rolling around, the three people on the bus hovered in the aisles spread-eagled, using every limb and joint to brace, support, grab, or stabilize the babies during the trip to the airport.

Later, LeAnn would recount that it was reminiscent of the famous chocolate factory scene in *I Love Lucy*.

Once the first one hundred babies were at the airport, other questions sprang up. How do you transport one hundred babies on an Air Force C-141 cargo jet? The aircrew put their creativity in action and gathered dozens of small cardboard boxes, big enough to fit two to three babies per box. Then, they used one long strap to serve as a giant seat belt for twenty-two boxes of babies at a time. Voilà, a new method of rapid baby transport created "on the fly." Literally.

How do you feed and care for one hundred babies with only nine in-flight volunteers? Answer: Create an ongoing assembly line, walking down the row of babies, propping bottles on the shoulders of box mates for feeding time, then picking them up for burping, then diaper changing. Lots and lots of diaper changing. The babies were stressed, fussy, and had diarrhea from the experience, which was a dehydration risk. So, more feeding. And more diapers changed. They finally arrived at Clark AFB in the Philippines, and some staff went back to rescue two hundred more babies. Then, two days later, all three hundred infants finally flew to the United States on a 747. This flight, each baby had their own seat— and cardboard box—so the babies all flew first-class.

Saigon fell three weeks later.

Six different organizations made Operation Babylift a success in a dark time, eventually rescuing three thousand babies out of Vietnam before it fell to the Communists of North Vietnam. Out of the three hundred babies LeAnn's group saved, all were adopted by loving families in America within a month.

LeAnn went on to be a career nurse, brilliant speaker, and bestselling author of *Chicken Soup for the Nurse's Soul.* In 1999, *Newsweek* did a "Voices of the Century" edition and in the section on the Vietnam War, opposite Henry Kissinger's photo, was a young, energized LeAnn in a VW van, surrounded by babies and showing a resolve and warrior spirit that said, "We got this."

-'-

LeAnn's story is a beautiful and compelling reminder that where there's a will, there is often a way (and hopefully some cardboard boxes and a VW van). But how many times do we forget this when faced with a seemingly impossible task? How often do we have the available resources on hand to accomplish the job but instead focus only on the things we lack?

Native American tribal communities were true experts at living off the land. Tribes throughout millennia used what was in their own backyard, literally, to create success. Our warriors could take the most basic of items—a rock, a stick, a bone—and creatively fashion an elegant, effective weapon that could take down an enemy in a fight or a moose during a hunt.

My people, the Ottawa Tribe (or Anishinaabe), used birchbark for housing, containers, and the canoes that made us successful in our area in trade and war. Beautifully crafted canoes had hulls less than a quarter inch thick, yet they were strong, fast, maneuverable, and light—a canoe eighteen feet long could weigh as little as thirty-five pounds. The Plains tribes, like the Lakota, used every part of the buffalo to make everything from clothing, bowstrings, and canteens to food and shelter. Pueblo peoples used local mud for adobe to make beautifully engineered multilevel apartment buildings that stayed cool in summer, warm in winter. Alaskan Natives, like the Inuit, used sealskin for clothing and boots. It's waterproof like Gor-Tex and warmer than other material, like cloth, at four times the thickness.

Tecumseh, the great Shawnee chief and warrior, said, "When you arise in the morning, give thanks for the morning light, for your life and strength. Give thanks for your food and the joy of living. If you see no reason for giving thanks, the fault lies with yourself." This isn't just a wonderful quote on gratitude. Tecumseh speaks to our ability to *see* the bounty in the first place.

When we see past our fear, resistance, and confusion, we realize we are all surrounded by an embarrassment of riches and resources. When we reframe our perspective, a whole world of possibility opens and we get unstuck from seeing only obstacles, limitations, and what we lack. We start seeing a world of wealth to draw from: our life, abilities, opportunities, other people, and technology. We start to see we're blessed beyond measure. In this moment. Be confident going forward and understand that you've got more than you'll ever need to create success in what you do available all around you—and in you—right now.

Warriors Think "Tribal-Centrically"

When we face challenges, sometimes fear and frustration get the best of us and we desperately ask ourselves, "What *do* I do?" But when you think tribal-centrically, a better question appears: "What *can* I do?" What do you have in your own backyard, in you and around you, to create a positive impact in your life and with others in your tribe? The truth is, you will never have all that you *want* to do your work—all the time, budget, support, or personnel. But if you think tribal-centrically about your resources, you often find you've got what you *need* to create success. And what you have is not nearly as important as how you use it. A rock is just a rock until you chip away and shape it into a useful arrowhead.

How do you use your precious and limited resources like time and energy each day? How do you use your skill sets, education, experience, training, knowledge, wisdom, attitude, work ethic, passion, and compassion on a daily basis to be even more effective? Think of a time in your life or career when you had a goal to achieve and very limited resources. What did you do and how did you make it work? What do you *wish* you would have had in that moment? What *did* you have in that moment?

When I started my business many years ago, I began with a passion to inspire people and help them create better lives for themselves. I had a business plan and drive but very few resources, no experience running a business, and little money to start. I *wish* I'd had a staff of experienced pros, a big office, a full technology suite, sophisticated marketing swag, a beautiful high-end website, and a razor-sharp assistant like Tony Stark had in *Iron Man*. Instead, what I *did* have was a Kinko's business card and a SkyPager. (Yep . . . a SkyPager.) That's what I started with, and everything grew from there. "Bloom where you are planted" doesn't just make a great bumper sticker. It's natural law and timeless wisdom.

Solutions can be as straightforward as we allow them to be, but we often get mixed up and emotionally charged from the challenge. Challenges makes us reexamine the question "Who and what am I willing to fight for?" Our warrior spirit is activated in those moments, now willing to overcome barriers, including our fear, pride, and ego. We're willing to sacrifice the time and energy required and push the limits of creativity, teamwork, and innovation. If you've ever watched *The Edge* with Sir Anthony Hopkins and Alec Baldwin, you know they had a serious problem. After a plane crash, which is terrible enough, the two found themselves stranded, cold, hungry, scared—and then being chased by an enormous and very hungry brown bear. They had no gear to speak of, not much skill, and little time to defend themselves. In the end, they used a pocketknife to fashion a long stick into a spear. The solution wasn't eloquent or expensive, and didn't require lots of know-how or time. But it worked. Not only did they kill the bear, but they also ate it and made clothes out of it. Nice. What can we learn from this? That:

- It's amazing to see what kind of solution we can create when we *need* to.

- Solutions need not be expensive, complicated, or showy. They just need to work!

- Sometimes huge challenges (made bigger by worry) require small solutions.

So, what do we *really* have to work with each day? Be clear-eyed about what you have access to and bring to the table each day. When we think about the resources at our disposal, we often jump to higher-level resources like technology, teammates, and the like—things outside of us. But the resources within us—the fundamentals of our time, energy, and personal "medicine bag" of gifts and skills—can be even more priceless and powerful when leveraged the right way.

Resource 1: Time

Time is the most important resource we have for two reasons.

First, how we spend our time defines every aspect of our lives. Our performance, health, happiness, relationships, success, and impact in serving others are all shaped by the time we invest or do not invest in those areas. The way we use our time counts for *everything*.

Two questions that can give us clarity on how we use our time:

1. Am I spending enough time on the things that matter?

2. Am I putting too much time into the things that don't?

If we never learn to distinguish which is which, we doom ourselves to daily chaos.

Second, it's nonrenewable. Every other resource, to some degree, can be resown, regrown, rebooted, or recharged. If our house burns down, we can build a new one. If we miss an opportunity, we can usually find or create a new one. If we lose a job, we can get another job. If we lose money, we can make more. If we experience a health crisis, we may usually recover. Heck, even if we lose love, we can find love again. That's what dating apps and dance clubs are for, right? But time spent is gone forever, so it's not just important, it is *absolutely critical* that we're putting it not toward *everything*, which is the temptation, but toward the *right* things.

A common excuse we've all used to avoid starting a project, improving ourselves, solving a problem, etc. is that we "don't have time." But if you could carve an extra thirty minutes of time from your day, where would you carve it from? Watching TV? Complaining or gossiping? The wrong answers include "driving to work faster" or "getting less sleep." (We'll talk about sleep shortly.)

Now that you have an extra thirty minutes, where would you put it? Toward family, wellness activities, reading, or hobbies? How do you think your life might look and feel if you did this for the next month? Or the next year?

Now, I've got good news and bad news when it comes to time. And like a good doctor, I'll give you the bad first. The bad news is that everyone and everything in the world wants your time. If we're not aware and vigilant, our time gets stolen away little by little. Think of the time we spend in lines. Or online. I'm not bashing technology, I use it every day, but it's simply a tool and needs to be used the right way. Just like a tomahawk is a tool, the way we use it determines the impact. You can use it to chop wood, strike an enemy with it, or bury it and make peace. It's just a tool.

Technology is great for transmitting data but limited when it comes to feeding relational connections. I've had many conversations with distraught folks who have a thousand Facebook friends and not one person with whom they feel they can be vulnerable, get coffee, or depend on in times of trouble. Just because we're plugged in does not mean we're connected. *Technology can enhance a relationship, but it should never be a substitute for one.* The line in our society regarding this is becoming blurred. We too often are cheapening one of the most sacred endeavors on our journey—the human-to-human relationship—by allowing it to be conducted by an app.

I had a conversation with a guy at a conference I'll never forget. Some other people and I were discussing the impact of digital media and games on our phones, including the game *Candy Crush*. At the mention of that game, the guy quickly slid into our group, eyes wide, and his hair even seemed to puff out. He reminded me of Kramer on *Seinfeld*. He eagerly told me how much he plays and how he just has to reach that next level. And the next. He plays it so much he forgot to pick his son up after soccer the week before. He then lowered his voice and told me seriously, "You've *got* to download it."

I'm not looking for a black hole to throw my time into, and I'm pretty sure you're not either. Entertainment and play are important for balance, but to be true warriors in our roles, we need to protect our time so we can put it where it counts.

Now, the good news about time is that because it is our most precious resource, it's also the most precious gift we can give anyone, including ourselves. A little bit can go a long way. Taking more time to invest in the important people in our lives doesn't require four hours of deep look-into-my-eyes time. A small bit, even a handful of seconds, given the right way, can change someone's life.

I've worked for many years in suicide prevention. Suicide has taken a devasting toll in our Native American communities and personally affected my life. I can't tell you how many times I've heard someone share heartbreaking words like this at conferences: "Eighteen years ago, I decided to end my life. I felt lost, hopeless, stuck. I felt that no one cared about me. And then I ran into [fill in the blank], who said [fill in the blank] to me, and it changed my mind." How many of those stories do we have to hear to know that a bit of time, given the right way, can change someone's life?

By the way, the stories are always the same. You can fill in the first blank with friend, coworker, uncle, cousin, teacher, etc. The second blank, what they said, is always just a few words, a story, or a check-in. It's never four hours of deep look-into-my-eyes time.

HOW TO GIVE THE GIFT OF TIME

But to make our time a "good give," a sincere offering that has real and positive impact, two things have to be honored.

The first is that we need to be *present* when we give our time. Presence is not just a warm body standing in front of a warm body, but the act of being there with our whole selves in all ways—physically, mentally, emotionally, and spiritually—even if it's for only a handful of seconds. This is the only way we can truly connect to someone in the moment, hear the unspoken, see the unshown, and vibe in their frequency. Our tribal elders teach us that giving someone your full attention honors them by showing respect.

The challenge of being present in our busy world is that we feel compelled to be constantly moving, constantly stimulated. And we can be, all too easily. Sometimes we're listening to our earbuds, watching a video, and eating a sandwich and wondering why we don't "connect" with that person who came to talk to us. *Presence* is bringing all of you into that moment, not only the parts that aren't engaged in watching a TikTok video. Connection requires presence, whether in person or online.

The second thing we need to do to make our gift of time count is that we must do it *willingly*. Have you ever had someone give you their time, but do it unwillingly or even with anger or grudgingly? How did it make you feel? Small, unimportant, angry, hurt, ignored, or worse? That is a laundry list of how we would never want someone to feel in our presence. We would never want them to feel those things when they're with us. Make a commitment to do what you can to ensure that when someone is with you, even for a handful of seconds, they don't feel dismissed, but feel honored. We create that by our willingness to show intentional attention. If we can make that one pivot in the way we relate to others, the quality of our relationships will go through the roof.

I had a moment where this broke down. One day, I went to a store and couldn't find what I was looking for. As I searched aisle after aisle, I found an employee I thought might be able to help me. She was on a personal phone call, and the volume of the conversation was what drew me to her from three aisles over. I looked up the aisle, waved my hand to let her know I was going to need help. The interaction went downhill from there.

Employee: "Shut up, she wasn't even at that party. That is so stupid, you're crazy!"

Me: Smiling and waving up the aisle at her to let her know I'll need some help.

Employee: Looks at me, rolls eyes, and lets out a long pfffffff. "I have to go . . . No, someone is here."

Me: Still smiling. Not waving. Starting to feel weird and out of place.

Employee: Visibly agitated. "No, he's *looking at me.* I'll call you back. Ha, ha, ha, you're so crazy!" Hangs up the phone, turns to me, stone-faced, and says with loud snark, "Can I help you?"

Now, she said the words, but would you feel you were going to be served well in that moment? I didn't either. Instead, I felt both those things I mentioned earlier: small and unimportant. That's the way we don't want to give our time. (By the way, people always try to get me to name the store where it happened and I'm not going to tell you that. But I'll give you a hint. It rhymes with *Schmalmart*. That's all I'm going to say.)

The point is, when we give our time grudgingly, people don't just see and hear it—they *feel* it—so we want to do our best to make sure we give even small bits of our time with willing heart.

And yes, I still enjoy shopping at Schmalmart as much as anyone, despite the isolated incident.

Now here's what a "good give" looks like. Several years ago, and before the place became King's Landing in *Game of Thrones*, some friends and I visited the beautiful city of Dubrovnik in Croatia. The place is famous for its simply prepared seafood, grilled with just olive oil and salt. But the challenge was that every restaurant served mostly the same items, which made it hard to decide where to eat dinner. Each evening, a few hours before dinner, people would sullenly offer colorful flyers to entice passersby to eat at their restaurant. After collecting a small stack, my group still couldn't decide.

Suddenly, and out of nowhere, a man jumped into our path

and energetically proclaimed, "Welcome to our restaurant! Please come in, the food is *delicious.*" He squeezed every bit of goodness out of that last word. Besides his big smile, I remember he had on pressed pants, a starched white shirt, and a napkin over his arm. "If you don't like the food here, I will buy it back and eat it myself!" Well, guess where we ate that night? Throughout the meal, he doted on us, asked about our backgrounds, shared history on the area, gave advice and the like. But what I remember, and will never forget, is the way we felt in his presence. He was with us for only small chunks of time, a few seconds here, a minute or two there, but each one felt sincere to the core, and we didn't just feel welcomed. We felt honored. We felt like family. I don't remember what I ate that night, but I will never forget the way "Mr. Delicious" made me *feel.*

Resource 2: Energy

Energy is a limited resource that should be rebooted and restored each day through diet, exercise, and especially sleep. The danger in trying to do too much lies in how it depletes our power and effectiveness. When we say, "I've got a million things to do today," we set ourselves up for overwhelm, and we *feel* it. It feels like we're too little peanut butter on too much toast. We're doing the worst thing a warrior can do in battle in those moments: We're dividing and conquering ourselves before the battle begins.

Like time, it's important not to put our energy toward *everything* but toward the right things. If we never determine which is which, we doom ourselves to chaos delivered daily. Not good. We'll talk later about figuring out your "right things" and what that looks like for you, but for now, let's talk about the best and healthiest way to replenish our energy: sleep.

Being ex-military and an avid reader of history, I've learned about the power and impact of sleep deprivation. I know that for hundreds of years it has been the most reliable form of torture. If experienced long enough, consistently enough, lack of sleep breaks us down physically, mentally, emotionally, and spiritually until we have nothing left to fight with. And all too often, we are doing it to ourselves.

Our elders in our tribal communities have always said, and still do, that the outdoors was our best classroom. Nature would teach us all we needed to be a happy, healthy human being. Well, the Max Planck Institute for Evolutionary Anthropology took our elders to heart and studied animals and their sleep patterns. A 2009 study published in *Discover* magazine found that the animals that got adequate sleep had six times the immunity cells in their bloodstreams. The animals that were sleep-deprived had twenty-four times the parasites. (Yuck!)

Now, what does that mean for us? If you go into work without enough sleep, are you going to get a tapeworm? Doubtful. I don't know who you work with, but it's highly unlikely. However, it doesn't mean we're not dealing with parasites daily. We are. A parasite is something that latches on to another living creature and slowly drains the life from them. We deal with that daily, in the form of negative people or situations, setbacks, confusion, disruptive change, and stress. Parasites can also come in the form of bad habits and practices that drain away our energy and optimism. We more effectively deal with all these situations and make better decisions toward them with a good night of sleep. It's free, doesn't require paperwork, enables us to be strong in our warrior role, and is one of the most important self-care choices we can make.

How many hours of sleep each night are recommended by doctors and scientists, on average, to be at our best the next day? The answer is seven to eight. (I had a guy in one of my programs a few years ago who said "thirteen." I stopped the program and asked, "Sir, are you a cat or toddler?") Now, let's be honest, thirteen sounds nice, but seven to eight hours of quality sleep is what we need. And yet most people do not get that each night. Some don't even come close. Yet we wonder why we feel depleted, run-down, foggy, and stressed and may inadvertently say something to someone else in a tense moment that we regret for a week.

Now, I know we all wish we could go back to naptime. When I was a kid, I hated naptime and would fight it all the way, throwing myself onto the floor in tears and wiggling like a worm on a skillet. Yet, I've had countless conversations with other hardworking professionals and realize most of us would give up an arm to have naptime come back. How awesome would that be? We're at work, eleven thirty rolls around, and we get issued our chocolate milk and sleeping mat and find the nearest corner to cuddle into. We may not ever get back to that place to recharge our sleep, but it doesn't mean we can't do that for ourselves each night.

The truth is, there is no time for anything in this world. No time to eat, work, play, spend with our loved ones, or sleep. There is *only* time for what we *make* time for, and if your health and wellness are not at the top of that pyramid, I'll tell you what you've also probably experienced. Your warrior spirit starts to evaporate, and all you're trying to do in your warrior role may fall short. How realistic is it to go into your life, relationships, and responsibilities and want to give one hundred percent of who you are and what you can do on a half-charged battery? Or less? That's like planting carrot seeds and hoping coconuts grow. It's a total disconnect from reality and we're out of alignment in that moment, operating in a way that will not achieve the results we're after. Only we can fix that.

Resource 3:
Our Personal Medicine Bag

In Native American culture, a medicine bag is filled with sacred, meaningful items—such as herbs like tobacco and cedar, beads, bones, arrowheads, stones, and animal claws or teeth—that hold power of protection, strength, good luck, or healing for the person who carries it. These medicine bags were often worn around the neck every day and became especially meaningful before and after ceremonies, battle, or illness. The medicine bag brings a sense of peace and confidence to the wearer since she knows she carries things with her that give her power and ability.

I'd like you to visualize a medicine bag you carry with you now and for the rest of your life. It's filled with all the things that make you uniquely and powerfully you in this world, impressive tools and gifts that we so often take for granted. They can be your natural talent and abilities, attitude, values, work ethic, and the priceless life lessons you've learned the hard way. We so often focus on what we lack, what we didn't get or never learned, and not nearly enough time on what we actually *have*. Everyone, including you, has a medicine bag filled with powerful items. What's in yours?

I do a "gift exchange" exercise in my programs, where I have people identify the special qualities that go in their medicine bags. Then I have them exchange a few of their "gifts" with others in the group. What I've found is that when people really recognize and *see* what they have to work with, they become very proud of and possessive about them. And they should be! These are innate abilities, natural talents, and the skills they've worked hard at for years to earn, develop, or strengthen. People start going from a mindset of "I really don't have anything special about me" to one that screams "I will not trade these for *anything* someone else has." I've seen people get defensive, picky, and even refuse to trade anything—and remember, this is a hypothetical exercise. They're not really giving up anything, but the emotions ignite regardless. Like

Gollum in *Lord of the Rings*, they huddle over their special gifts, mumbling, "Myyyy precioussssss . . ."

At the end of the day, you've been gifted with innate talents and abilities and have earned your skill sets, education, experience, and wisdom. So be aware and proud of what you have to work with—and use it all. It really is precious! And the good news is that we don't have to trade any of our current gifts or skills to add or develop new ones.

And just as important as the skills you have is *how* you use them every day. After all, how many primary colors are there? Only three—and yet those three can be used and combined to create a masterpiece in painting. How many basic notes are there in a musical scale? Only seven—and yet, those few notes have created songs that have endured in our tribal communities for millennia. How many letters in the English alphabet? Those twenty-six letters have written pieces that have moved millions to action. The point is *what* we have isn't nearly as important as *how* we use what we have.

I'm passionate about this idea for two reasons.

The first is because I've witnessed it countless times in my travels over two decades, seeing examples of small groups throughout our tribal communities—or even individuals—with few resources that are making magic happen in serving their tribe. What they don't have in physical resources they more than make up for with their grit, creativity, teamwork, commitment to their mission, and showing strong examples of the warrior spirit at work. I'm constantly inspired by them and they fuel my work and belief in these principles.

Sonya Tetnowski (Makah Tribe) is the CEO of the Indian Health Center of Santa Clara Valley (IHCSCV) and a U.S. Army Airborne veteran. She is a warrior through and through, dedicated to serving others. Unfortunately, her caring staff at IHCSCV are always stretched, and resources always scarce, as they serve twenty-three thousand patients annually. So it was an unpopular move when Sonya decided to add trainings in emergency management and practice drills for mass distribution of food and supplies, including vaccinations, to her staff's already full workload. But Sonya knew in her gut that it was the right investment of time, energy, and skills. And then COVID-19 hit.

Sonya told me, "When the virus was first announced in another country, I pulled my chiefs and directors together and started planning for it to arrive on our shores." It quickly became apparent that the tough choices she'd made to train her staff despite a shortage of resources were reaping huge dividends. IHCSCV was the first in the county to set up an emergency operations center and stockpile supplies it would need. Before the pandemic hit, Sonya and her team did a financial assessment and stopped the purchase of a building, froze hiring, and minimized expenditures, knowing they'd need all available cash for what was coming.

Sonya says, "We had fully trained safety officers, distribution hubs, and emergency supplies in various locations. We were the first to set up drive-through testing and mass vaccination events in our county. It paid off to plan and prepare so everyone knew exactly what to do and when to do it. Our first dose was administered on December eighteenth, 2020, months ahead of any other clinic in our county."

The effectiveness of IHC of Santa Clara Valley became a blueprint of success, and Sonya and her team began training other urban health sites on how to deliver vaccines quickly, safely, and in mass numbers. Their great investment of time, energy, and skill benefited not just their patients but all the other patients in all the other sites they worked with.

The second reason I'm passionate about this idea is that I'm a living, walking realization of this concept. When I was born, my parents were teenagers in poverty. Everything they had could fit into the trunk of a car. And they didn't own a car. They'd make one meal, eat it all week. They read to each other each night for entertainment because they didn't have money for a TV. I benefited from that tremendously, even though the first book read aloud was Mario Puzo's *The Godfather*. I slept in a dresser drawer the first three months of my life and when I did get a crib, my mom put the baby face from the Pampers box next to it to keep me company. I gurgled and cooed at the image for hours, my first audience.

Thinking tribal-centrically and leveraging my time, energy, and what was in my medicine bag for many years, I ended up in Washington, DC, to do a keynote program. I was being checked in by a security officer with a submachine gun over his shoulder. He found my name on the list, looked up at me with a grin, and said, "Welcome to the White House, Mr. Vanas." I can't put that moment into words. I don't even try. The point I do try to make is simply this: It doesn't matter who you are, where you come from, or what you have. What matters is how you *honor* who you are and where you come from by *using* what you have every day.

⁎

Let's end this chapter with ice cream. In 2011, a massive earthquake triggered a tsunami that hit Japan. Vast fields of strawberries were flooded and destroyed. The fruit now too ravaged and unappealing to sell, the farmers were devastated and depressed, but they refused to quit. After all, they had families and workers to take care of, so they recruited help from a pastry chef to see if there were any creative ways to salvage the crop.

The chef had an idea to liquefy the strawberries into a dessert topping, but found it would solidify instantly when added to cream. In his frustration, he turned to a pharmacy professor at Kanazawa University, whose team found that it did make a terrible topping, but a compound found in the liquid from strawberries, polyphenol, was a perfect binding agent. From this, Kanazawa ice cream pops were created, which stay frozen for over an hour at room temperature. These resilient people utilized the warrior spirit at work, refused to quit, and instead found a way through force of will to act, be creative, and find a way to make success from a tsunami. They turned bad fruit into a great product.

We've identified our basic resources of time, energy, and the riches in our medicine bags. Together, the three form a "trifecta of goodness" in the shape of an arrowhead. And we're firing off those arrows daily. Are you shooting them purposefully, at targets you choose, or in every direction into the wind and hoping they hit something? That question brings us to the next chapter, where we'll explore aligning our resources with what is important, so we start creating success in our daily shots, make good trades, and start seeing the impact of warrior spirit at work.

3

Prepare for Battle

Vision Questing for Life

I sat slumped over in place as my body jackhammered in the frozen dark. I was soaked, dehydrated, and felt cold to the core of my throbbing bones. Through a stuffy nose, I could still smell the damp earth and pine needles all around me. I was halfway through a four-day vision quest ceremony. I wore only shorts and was wrapped in a soaked blanket, cradling my prayer pipe in my arm. This was my fourth and final year. I had prepared my mind and spirit for many moons to be ready for this ceremony, but now that I was in it, I was struggling. I wondered if I'd be able to make it through. The question spun in my mind like a caged hummingbird.

The vision quest ceremony is a traditional rite of passage that many tribes practice to guide individuals to seek clarity, guidance, and direction in life—or prepare for a tough time or battle. We did ours in the spring to help prepare ourselves to face the grueling experience of the Sun Dance, which happens later in the summer. Our traditional tribal ceremonies often require deprivations like the ones we endure on a vision quest to pull away the physical trappings that occupy our minds and transport us into a spiritual place. No food. No water. No shelter. Just you, your prayer pipe, and a blanket in an area the size of a tabletop in the wilderness. Alone.

We prepared for the vision quest with a purification ceremony in the sweat lodge, or inipi. We wore only our shorts and an eagle feather in our hair as we each cradled our pipe and crawled into the lodge in a sacred, humble way. On our hands and knees. That's the only way in and that is by design. Humility is the great equalizer and shows us that we are all human beings, capable of great things as well as mistakes. Forever perfectly imperfect.

My spiritual leader and I sat quietly as the heated stones, the "old ones," were brought into the center by the firekeeper. Our leader sprinkled dry cedar buds that crackled on the hot rocks and filled the lodge with a tangy smoke. The bucket of water was brought in and blessed. He closed the flap of the lodge and the ceremony began. The thick perfume scents of cedar, sage, and sweetgrass hung heavy in the air and were joined by the loud hiss of the water pouring over the glowing rocks. We sang the first prayer songs and invited the spirits into the lodge. The hot steam washed over our bodies and the complete darkness took away our eyesight and opened the eye of our hearts. I always feel security and comfort in a lodge, which represents being back in the womb.

As the flap was raised, the light rushed in and traded places with the billowing steam. We crawled out and stood, feeling naked and reborn as the vapors rose off our bodies in the dying sunlight. This was the first step in melting away the negative energies of doubt, fear, and worry to prepare for our vision quest so we could be open to the guidance we sought. In the next step, I was placed in the wilderness as the sun slipped beneath the trees. Once I was alone, I began the prayers that would last for four days. The darkness brought the thunder, and the thunder brought the rain . . .

The Lakota call the traditional rite of vision quest Hanblecheyapi, which means "to cry for a vision." You don't really understand why it's called that until you go on yours. Every year of my vision quest was difficult. Every year I suffered. Whether it was the extreme heat or cold, the rain or wind, insects, intense dehydration, or loneliness, every year I was tested to my limits no matter how much I'd prepared. I endured over one-hundred-degree heat one year, the next brought freezing cold, the next had epic nonstop insect attacks, and during my fourth year I was wet, cold, and surrounded by lightning strikes for most of the four days. The answers I sought didn't arrive in a bolt of lightning, in a sacred dream, or through the words of a prophet. It was more like a slow, penetrating smile that spreads across the face of a person who realizes they're the victim of a practical joke. Sometimes the most obvious things are the hardest to see.

Every year I learned more about myself and the world around me. I learned that life is simple. I learned that it's vital we understand where we're going and why. Each time I went to seek a vision, I felt pushed beyond my limits and got new clarity. The complication and confusion of everyday life melts away and leaves only the thoughts of what is truly important and matters. When I was lonely, hungry, cold, hot, thirsty, afraid, or in pain, I didn't think about taxes, car payments, career moves, or politics. I thought about water, food, shelter, family, and friends. I thought about why I'm here in the first place.

We do our best to make life complicated and unfortunately, we do a great job. We create artificial needs and requirements for happiness when everything we could ever hope for may already be there. Each ceremony, I was amazed at how little we really need in this life to be happy. I have seen grown men cry after drinking a cup of water after thirsting for several days. I have seen hugs between family members after a ceremony that seemed as if they would never end. Not once have I ever seen a person run to get their cell phone and call the office after standing on the line between life and death.

Vision is such a vital concept among tribal communities that it is seen as sacred—that's why we have ceremonies like the vision quest that facilitate this discovery process. The good news is, you don't have to go on a traditional vision quest to receive or create a vision for your life, but to consistently deliver in your role and serve others, you do have to spend time figuring out what yours is and why it matters.

We're ineffective as warriors in our roles when we don't know what we're fighting for or why it matters to us. It's a quick recipe to create confusion and deplete our warrior spirit. When we don't know where we're going, it's easy to get distracted from serving others, to waste time and energy on the frivolous, or to let the wrong things (like greed, power, or adulation) drive us. When we know what matters, we have a clear direction on how to best use the precious time on our journey. Fear will still be present, but our purpose becomes bigger than our fear, which enables us to focus more on what we are trying to do and less on what might be holding us back.

Our warriors had clarity of purpose: to serve their tribe. Before battle, they would reaffirm their purpose to maximize their chance at success by spending time in prayer or ceremony, fasting, preparing their weapons and gear, and checking on the younger warriors. They also used their medicines or made offerings, which could include burning sage, sweetgrass, or cedar or offering tobacco or corn pollen, to clean away negative energy and ask for the blessing of protection from the Creator. The final preparations could be applying war paint on their bodies, faces, and even their horses for protection and strength and to intimidate their enemy.

We prepare for our own battles by first getting clarity on our values and what we value. These serve as signposts pointing toward the vision we're trying to create on our journey and the story we tell about it to others—and ourselves.

Let's Talk about
Values—and What We Value

If vision is the picture we're painting on the canvas, then values, and what we value, are the colors. One builds into the other. When we know what those values and what we value look like for us, everything in life becomes easier. We know what to say yes to, and equally important, if not more so, we know what to say no to as well. We have clarity in a world of chaos—a wonderful gift to ourselves—and now know where to make our commitments, spend our time, and use our energy.

Alaska is one of my favorite places to visit. Each time I go, I fall in love again with the people, the culture, and the natural beauty of the environment. If you've ever been to Alaska, you know that the farther from Anchorage you go, the smaller the airplanes get. You arrive in a giant Airbus, but on that last leg of the journey out to the villages where I do most of my work, you take a small plane or boat.

Years ago, I traveled to a village just like that called Nanwalek. I was in a tiny airplane, a single-engine four-seat Cessna. My village point of contact was in the copilot seat and I was in the back with all the gear. Anytime a small plane travels out to a village, it's loaded with everything possible because no one knows when they'll be able to make it out there again. So, I'm in the back with all kinds of random things: baby shoes, cell phones, house paint, peanut butter, etc. I felt like I was in an Indiana Jones movie.

The pilot was from a traditional Russian community, which they still have in Alaska since it used to be a Russian territory. He fit the bill perfectly. Ice-blue eyes. Russian accent. Big fur hat with giant earflaps. We were having a great conversation and I looked down at the village where we were about to land. And I got nervous. Really nervous. As I pointed down, I asked, "Are you going to try and land there?" He chuckled and said in his heavy accent, "Yes, yes, my friend, conditions are perfect." In my mind, I yelled, "Look at the runway, man!" It was dirt, looked about a hundred yards long, and from my perspective had the slight shape of a banana and ran right against the crashing ocean. I clutched the house paint and peanut butter like they were life itself. He dropped the flaps, kicked over the rudder, and pulled off a landing smoother than butter on toast.

We got out of the Cessna and as we unloaded, I was amazed by how much cargo came out of this tiny airplane. It was like a clown car; each time I was sure it was empty, another something came out. I looked at the pilot in amazement and asked, "How on earth did you fit all of that stuff in that tiny airplane?" He looked at me and chuckled again. "Yes, yes, we pack everything but the chicken sink."

Yes, he actually said "chicken sink." And I laughed about that for three days. On the way home, I reflected how often we follow the same dynamic in our lives. We pack everything but the "chicken sink" and wonder why we have such a hard time getting and staying airborne. It's not just knowing what to say yes to but what to say no to as well. Saying no to gossip sessions around the breakroom or to struggling needlessly alone allows us to say yes to getting tasks done and to seeking answers or guidance from others. We have clarity on what matters to us when we consciously choose our values and what we value. And if we're pursuing targets that aren't in alignment with what matters to us, then we're expending all our great resources in wrong directions. Clarity counts toward our ability to effectively create our life.

What are your values? What do you value? These are two of the most important questions we will ever ask ourselves. Our values and what we value are a guiding force in determining the quality of our life and how we serve others. There is great risk in not determining what those are. We live in a society that is all too eager to tell us what our values should be. We're bombarded from every direction by messages that tell us what to think, feel, do, and be. Many of those messages promote instant gratification, image over substance, drama, and gain of money or fame at any cost. If we haven't decided on our values, the messages we get from media may start looking more and more attractive in the absence of our own better choices.

When we know our values, things such as love, service, integrity, or fortitude, we have the basic elements of our own version of a "good life." *What* we value are things like our health, family, career, culture, or community.

Determining what our values and what we value are begins with letting go of the negativity that takes up so much of our energy. The first step in most traditional ceremonies across Indian Country involved a purification or cleansing process.

This was done in a variety of ways, like fasting or burning medicines as mentioned above, but it was always done for the same reason: to sweep away all the clutter and negative energy, including the doubt, fear, anger, regret, worry, shame, and confusion that we all carry around with us in spiritual backpacks that weigh nine hundred pounds. We get to drop that backpack from our shoulders, get back to solid ground and the things that matter. We're able to enter the circle with an open heart and mind and get so much more out of that experience because of it. We can do this for ourselves, sweep away the clutter to regain clarity, each day, when we know what matters to us.

Values provide us with a center point, an anchor, something to return to after every hardship, over and over again, to keep moving forward. Within our Anishinabek tribal communities, the Seven Grandfather Teachings are paramount: love, honesty, truth, bravery, wisdom, respect, and humility. This is the recipe for a "good life." The Diné or Navajo people adhere to a value of hózhó, harmony or balance, and follow the wonderful life advice of "walking in beauty." Warrior societies from every tribal nation incorporated the values of courage, commitment, and service above all else. They understood that their role was not to feed and protect their egos but to feed and protect the people. These are enduring value systems that sustained our tribes and strengthened our warriors through the worst of times, including famine, disease, genocide, warfare, dislocation, and trauma. The point here is that things built on clear, compelling values tend to last—and succeed. When you build your life on the foundation of your values, you're able to do the same.

Any values-based culture, including our tribal nations, considers living its values as the highest form of success. Knowing our values enables us to "walk our talk." We're able to create alignment between the values we choose and the actions we take—and we breathe life into them when we do. We can't say we value integrity if we don't do what we say we'll do; we can't say we value excellence if we don't hold high standards for ourselves. Living our values may not have anything to do with the car we drive or how much money we make or awards we receive. If we're living our lives in alignment with the values we've chosen, we're already succeeding each day.

Vision: The First Step in Every Creation

Once we know our values and what we value, we can create the vision that feeds and sustains the things most important to us. If you know that service is one of your highest values, then that will be vital when you answer other meaningful questions: What kind of life do you want to create? What kind of career are you trying to build? When we incorporate our values and what we value into these answers, we have alignment between intentions and actions and know where to put our precious time, energy, and the gifts we carry in our medicine bag. If we don't get this right, our life will be like filling a cracked pot with water—no matter how much we put into it, it will still feel empty. This can happen when we chase the wrong vision (or someone else's) or cave to peer or societal pressures instead of following our own path.

Vision is the first step in every creation and can include our lives and careers. The first step in building a house isn't a group of eager workers showing up with lumber, tools, and doughnuts. Someone, somewhere, saw the vision in their mind first. Sight is what we see with our eyes, but vision is what we see with our minds. Once the person sees it in their mind, they can create a blueprint, figure out a budget and timeline, gather materials and personnel, and make it reality. The miracle behind the power of vision is that before they cut the first board or lay the first brick, they know exactly what the place will look like. That is how vision works.

Maybe your goal is to create a health/wellness group at your company. What would be its purpose, what activities could you do, what benefits would it provide to those who participate? Start to create the vision in your mind first, of how it would look, feel, and operate. Then, finding out the process to create a group, drafting a game plan, promoting interest, and scheduling the first meeting are actions that breathe life into the vision.

A Pueblo elder named Isabel once told me about the traditional Concho ways of the Pueblo people. She said that in celebration of the new year, people would make little clay shapes of the things they wanted to see in their lives. A baby. A deer for a good hunt. Their ancestors understood the connection between what's in our minds and what emerges in our world through our intentional actions. What does that look like for you on the journey ahead?

BREATHING LIFE INTO A VISION

We often overlook how vision can change our work and the way we serve others. Julie Garreau (Cheyenne River Mnicoujou Lakota) is a rock star in my book when it comes to vision. The spirits agree. Her given name in ceremony is Touches the Stars Woman, and she honors that name by living up to it. In 1988, at the age of twenty-one, she pursued a vision to serve her community and provide a healthy, safe place for youth in Eagle Butte, South Dakota, on the Cheyenne River Sioux Reservation, a hardscrabble community that has many of the social issues we see too much of across Indian Country—poverty, violence, substance abuse, and suicide. Julie came from a service-oriented family, the daughter of a father who served in law enforcement and a mother who was the executive director of the Elderly Nutrition Center.

With a strong vision, self-belief, and the will to see it through, Julie started the first iteration of the Cheyenne River Youth Project (CRYP), known as "The Main," in a defunct, decrepit bar called the Little Brown Jug on Main Street. Despite setbacks, doubts, lack of resources, and little support, Julie stayed focused on her vision, feeling that the positive impact it could have was worth fighting for. She quickly discovered how much she loved the work and the kids she was serving as well as being with the volunteers she gathered. Julie felt overwhelmed and realized she needed to strategically partner with benevolent forces, funders, and more volunteers to create it.

From those humble beginnings, Julie honored and fulfilled that vision to what CRYP is today, a stellar model youth program. CRYP has a five-acre comprehensive campus that includes multiple youth centers for different ages, a community garden, an e-store, a gift shop, food distribution, and many family and school support programs as well as ones that promote arts, crafts, and literacy. They host large-group activities such as Midnight Basketball and Passion for Fashion, and more targeted programs such as teen internships in art, social enterprise, Native wellness, Native food sovereignty, and Indigenous foods and cooking. They're in the process of building a physical home for the Lakota Youth Arts & Culture Institute.

Through funding issues, staff challenges, COVID, and the economic hardships, Julie and her CRYP continue to find ways to keep moving forward and fulfilling the vision. As she told me:

> I take my responsibilities very seriously, because a lot of kids are relying on us, and that means everything. It's my life's work. I've learned that our Lakota values are priceless tools you carry with you all the time. Be courageous, wise, generous, compassionate, and honest—rely on your values.

CRYP is, has been, and always will be a place where our Lakota youth can learn, discover, connect, have fun, and be safe. They actually envision a future in which they do more than survive. They thrive. Whatever needs to happen, I'll make happen. I don't feel like a visionary; I just care about my community and want to do more.

Spoken like a true visionary.

VISION KILLERS: THE THINGS THAT GET IN THE WAY

For every great idea we have, for every vision we create, there will be a critic, circumstance, or challenge that will stand in the way of creating it. One of the biggest threats to our vision is pushing through the notorious f-word we try to avoid. Fear. For many of us, especially as we get older and more seems at stake, creating a vision gets harder and the realities of life and career start getting in the way.

When we are little kids, we are all visionaries, seeing the world as it truly is—full of possibilities and potential. Ask kids between four and six years old what they want to do when they grow up, they'll say everything under the sun: basketball player, teacher, superhero, doctor, etc. My goal when I was four was to be a fire truck. Luckily, our goals adjust over time. Then we start going to school and hearing things like "no," or "that idea is goofy," or listening to other kids who don't know any more about life than we do. Nasty comments that may come later, like "No one's ever done that, what makes you so special?" and "Who do you think you are?" can trigger debilitating doubt. Then we're limping out of high school or college with our vision in tatters. Or gone. Those things we were most passionate about can get covered over with criticism, fear, or disappointment.

My friend John is Chickasaw, from a little town called Wetumka in the great state of Oklahoma. When John was eight years old, he would sit in a cardboard box and dream of blasting off into space. You could imagine the heckling that idea may have stirred up—barbs like "There're no Indian astronauts," or "You're from a small town in Oklahoma no one's heard of," or "That'll never work." It may have generated harsh questions like "Who do you think you are?" and "What makes you so special?"

When John finished high school, he decided to try college, but his heart wasn't in it. His interests were in the mountains, rock climbing, and not in the classroom. At the end of his first year, he pulled a 1.7 GPA and was suspended from the university. Off he went to join a survey crew in Colorado that was working on the I-70 corridor in Glenwood Canyon. Luckily, John's boss became a mentor. He pulled him aside one day and asked, "John, what do you want to do with the rest of your life?" John hadn't thought about it for some time and said, "I don't know. I guess this." His boss interjected, "No, you're smart, you're talented, you can do whatever you put your mind to."

That triggered John to harken back to the vision he'd had so long ago. He decided to go back to school and graduated. His final year he tutored a retired Navy captain, in calculus, who tutored him in a Navy career. He followed the man's advice and became a commissioned officer, an aviator, and a test pilot in the Navy. He went on to get his master's in aeronautical engineering and applied twice to NASA. And in 1996, U.S. Navy Commander John B. Herrington of the Chickasaw Nation became our country's first Native American astronaut. Among many items representing his Native American heritage, an eagle feather flew out of Earth's atmosphere on his mission. I saw him ten months before he went up in the Space Shuttle *Endeavour* in 2002 and I swear I could see the excited eyes of an eight-year-old beaming from John's face.

The thing that I've found is that no matter how small or big your vision, there will always be a knuckleheaded naysayer who will tell you why you can't, shouldn't, or won't fulfill it. Whether it's trying to improve a system at work, writing a book, going back to school, or becoming an astronaut, those people will show up. Don't let them talk you out of your vision. Or they will.

We see how vision can change the world. One of my favorite examples of this is that of the Wright brothers. As a lifelong aviation and space travel fan, Orville and Wilbur continue to inspire me. Imagine, two brothers from a small town in Ohio, high school dropouts, owned a bike shop, put their heads together, and created something that flew under its own power. I imagine how the conversation might have been via text:

Orville: Hey, Wilbur, I've got an idea. Let's build something in the garage that we can fly!

Wilbur: That sounds crazy, bro. We make bikes.

Orville: Yeah, we could build it out of, I don't know, like chicken wire, wood, and maybe cloth. Then we strap an engine on it. C'mon, this will be really cool! It could change the world . . . and you can go first!

Wilbur: WTF???

But they did and it did change the world. It ushered in the age of aviation, then the space age, and then the age of computers. What a way to serve humanity! It all started with a vision and then they breathed life into it with their actions. And yes, although Orville is credited with the first controlled, powered flight of an airplane, Wilbur did go first, but his attempt ended in failure.

Sometimes the biggest challenges to seeing our vision through come from those closest to us. A great example of this comes from Sequoyah of the Cherokee Nation. In the early 1800s, Sequoyah had a vision that the future of his people would be found in the "talking leaves"—reading and writing— but the Cherokee people did not have a written language system. So he set out to create one. It wasn't easy. In fact, he became so obsessed with the vision that he started to let his fields go fallow and stopped spending time with his friends. His wife thought she'd help put an end to this craziness and get Sequoyah to return to normal by throwing all he'd worked on into the fire! But it didn't stop him, and he developed a written Cherokee syllabary. By the 1830s the Cherokee people were one of the most literate groups in America. Not just among tribal communities in America, but in America as a whole! They published the first Native American newspaper, the *Cherokee Phoenix*, and it is still in print today. That is the power of a vision realized, even when those closest to us reject it.

A Good Trade

Every day of our lives we are trading our time, focus, and effort to get something in return—hopefully results that bring our vision into reality. Doing that requires a strategic sacrifice of our resources and sometimes other possibilities or directions. We can't do it all, so we must choose consciously. We can trade our time, energy, and skills to complain, worry, gossip, continue bad habits, or participate in the frivolous or petty—but we can also trade that time and effort to improve relationships, our wellness, the way we serve, and our skill sets or knowledge base. But every day the great exchange continues, and the results of how we're trading show up in our lives and careers, indicating whether we're doing it well or need to improve.

Before Europeans made it to the shores of Turtle Island (aka North America) there was no standard currency throughout Native communities, and it was all based on the barter and exchange of goods that were worthy of trade. Give up one thing to get something else. We traded beaver pelts for things like metal hatchets, copper pots, and cloth and facilitated trade among the other tribes and the Dutch, English, and French as well. And my people were excellent traders, real pros. In fact, it's how we got our name, Ottawa. It sprang from a miscommunication related to that endeavor.

Our tribe ranged all throughout modern-day Michigan and southern Ontario, Canada, trading on the rivers and lakes with our brilliantly crafted canoes. When the French came and "discovered" us in the early 1600s, we had a vibrant, successful trade network set up with all the tribes in the area. When the French saw this, they were impressed—and a little jealous too. I always pictured the Frenchmen in big hats with peacock feathers, white tights, buckle shoes . . . I don't know that they were wearing these things, but that's the movie I play in my mind. They asked our people a simple question. "Who are you?" Well, we didn't speak French and they didn't speak our language, so we misunderstood and thought they asked, "What are you doing?" So we answered and said *odawa*, which means "to trade." The French said, "Sacré bleu, you'll be 'Odawa'" (also now known as Ottawa). We still call ourselves Anishinaabe, which means "the people."

What a dumb way to get named as a group, named after the first thing they catch you doing. That could've been much worse (think about it). But I digress.

Each day, this trade dynamic is a constant. Just as we give our money in exchange for a Starbucks latte, we are trading our good stuff mentioned in chapter 2, for something in return. The great exchange is a daily constant and it's not about pure productivity either. Sometimes the best trades we make are exchanging a few hours for a hike, less TV for more sleep, or more family time in place of time on social media. In these moments, we're able to recharge our warrior spirit and strengthen ourselves.

We can't say yes to everything, or we become overwhelmed and not able to create our visions. So, when we say yes, we want to mean it. I've found that when we're constantly saying yes to *everything*, we're really saying yes to *nothing*. It's like being at an all-you-can-eat buffet and you never say no to anything. What happens? You come back to your table with a plate of food three feet high. We set ourselves up for overwhelm. Sometimes "no" is a complete sentence, and we must practice saying it more, or else we don't say "yes" enough to the things that fuel our vision.

Especially for those warriors who proudly serve others, who express their warrior spirit through work in service to others, "no" can be the hardest word to say. "No" feels like a violation of our commitment. "No" feels like we're letting others down. I know how it feels. We'd rather take on almost any "yes" than say no. Even if that yes depletes us, divides us, and leads us to overwhelm or to that martyr role I mentioned before. If we don't keep the vision of what we're trying to do clear in our minds, then saying no will always make us feel guilty, ashamed, or angry with ourselves to such a degree that we'll find a way to slide into an "almost no," which is a "sideways yes."

For instance, let's say you're already fully scheduled and need to complete a project due at the end of the day. Someone comes in and asks you to read over and edit a ten-page document right now because they have a meeting at the end of the day. You say you're too busy. They give you a sad look. You say you're fully scheduled and just can't do it. They stand there, waiting. You finally cave to the pressure and say, "Well, I can't do it right now, but guess I can at least read it over during my lunch." Then you do it, but you're frustrated that you agreed. Sound familiar? Be aware that saying yes when we don't want to (or don't really mean it) can also set us up to harbor resentment toward the person we said yes to. That is a quick way to feeling bad and confused at the same time.

I'm not saying don't help others; that is the antithesis of the warrior role we've explained. All or nothing is seldom a wise approach to anything in life. What I'm saying is that there needs to be balance, and erring on the side of "no" gives us healthy room to better figure out what we want to say "yes" to. Without pressure, confusion, or resentment.

What *Ghostbusters* Can Teach Us about Vision

A quick way to lose clarity in working toward our vision can happen when we "cross the streams." When we're at work, we're ruminating about home and when at home, we're obsessing about work. In that scenario, we're not fully engaged or effective in either space. Our vision for both is muddled and out of focus, and becomes much harder to achieve. I asked this question two paragraphs earlier.

One of my favorite movies, the original *Ghostbusters* starring Dan Aykroyd and Bill Murray, had a great concept that can help us maintain clarity on our visions. The characters carried proton packs that would shoot high-energy beams that could capture ghosts. Egon, the designer of the weapon, issued a grave warning. "Do not cross the streams." Why? Because "bad things could happen."

In our own lives, we experience the same when we cross the streams of work and home life. When we're at work, we should work. When we work hard, work with focus, stay solution-oriented, and use our time wisely, we realize the vision of a productive day. And when we're at home, we should be at home. When we rest, relax, play, and reconnect with the crazy people called family and friends who invigorate and love us through it all, we allow the vision of a full recharge and rejuvenation to emerge. When we violate this and cross the streams, bad things happen.

4

Count Coup on the Enemy

Facing and Defeating Fear

t was a summer day in Colorado and the sound of the wind stream and roaring engines was deafening. I shuffled a handful of feet toward the open door, but it felt like miles. We were in a De Havilland Twin Otter aircraft 4,800 feet above the ground. I was standing in the doorway of the airplane when I looked where I shouldn't have: down. Even over the loud drone and vibration of the engines, I could still feel my heart beating out of my chest.

I'd just finished an intensive two-week training at the U.S. Air Force Academy Jump School Program, the only certified jump program in the world where students make their first freefall jump without any assistance. Now me and my "stick," or jump group of about a dozen, were about to leap from a perfectly good airplane. No static line or tandem jumps. Just ten seconds of freefall from an altitude of five thousand feet, where you got to contemplate every decision you'd ever made while screaming, praying, and begging for your momma—all in one breath.

My fellow cadets and I'd trained intensely, practicing our jump sequences all day, every day. It got drilled into our heads so deeply that we would all joke at chow that we had dreamed about jump sequences at night. The reason for the repetition was so that we'd be able to rely on a clear and well-practiced plan and routine, and not our emotions, when it came time to do the real jump. Our emotions can lie to us, telling us things like "We should quit. It won't work. It's too hard, too scary." That is the f-word showing up in a big way: fear. It can shut us down in the moment we need to act. The structured, re-petitive training transformed the stress of what we were about to do into a casual boredom. That's when it became muscle memory and allowed us to show up and conquer our fear dur-ing this program.

The first person to make the jump was my roommate dur-ing the course, Charlie. I could see the terror in his eyes as he stood up and shuffled to the door. He looked back at me with eyes the size of saucers. Then the jumpmaster yelled "GO!" and out he went. I saw the glint of his helmet, the bottom of his combat boots, and swear I could hear him yell.

Next it was my turn. After seeing Charlie, I wished I would have been first. The jumpmaster came to me, pointed his fin-ger at me, and ordered, "STAND IN THE DOOR." I felt tempted to look around and ask, "Are you sure you mean me? Let's talk about this." Instead, I slowly stood on jellified legs and shuffled toward my doom. Looking back at my group, I saw some nods and one guy put a shaky hand forward with a wiggling thumbs-up, smiling as if to say, "Don't be chicken, we're going right after you."

The jumpmaster yelled "GO" and out the door I went. I hit the airstream and immediately went into a tumble. Sun, mountains, ground were what I saw in a repeating swirl. Fear arrived with the loud rush of wind in my ears. It was a full-blown experience of terror as I twisted and turned in freefall, like in a nightmare where you're falling into the abyss. My mind and body were buffeted into a state of overwhelm and I felt out of control. "Remember the training!" I finally yelled inside my head during the chaos.

In a second, I arched my whole body and got into a stable freefall position, went through my sequence, and pulled my rip cord. Out came a full and beautiful chute, slowing me down from 120 to about 15 mph in a second and a half. After the opening shock, I saw stars and danced in my harness, screaming with joy. The fact that I got blown out of the jump zone and across the main road and crashed into a small tree (didn't feel small when I hit it) did nothing to diminish the exhilaration I felt after completing the course. After that experience I felt I could do anything. I had faced and conquered my fear.

Courage is not the absence of fear, it is acting in the face of it. Going through the jump program made me realize how important training, repetitive practice, the right mindset, and being surrounded by the right people are in being able to deliver when I needed it. We will all face the hard things, the seemingly impossible things, that scare us to our core. How we respond in that moment often defines the outcome, so we've got to practice courage as often as possible to keep strengthening it. When we do that, it will serve us when we need it.

This process of accumulating courage during our jump program through small acts, training, familiarity, and practice was part of our Native traditions as well. Warriors weren't expected to display courage for the first time by jumping headlong into a pitched battle. Courage *was* expected and valued, so it was developed purposefully and practiced often, methodically and in stages, with ceremonies like the vision quest, and activities like the first hunt, the first raid, and then the first battle.

For example, the Plains tribes held a tradition in combat that was more honorable than killing an enemy on the battlefield. It was called "counting coup." Instead of striking their enemy down with an arrow, lance, or war club, they'd simply touch them with a coup stick, a decorated staff resembling a riding crop, while in the heat of battle. This was a courageous act of confronting the enemy face-to-face and in essence saying, "I'm not afraid of you." The ultimate act of bravery.

We must do the same to develop a warrior spirit in our lives. Count coup on fear by facing your own and acting anyway. That is courage in action. Exercising courage isn't just for jumping from a plane, running with the bulls, or swimming with sharks. We exercise and strengthen our courage when we do things that scare us on a regular basis, whether that's jumping headlong into a tough conversation, taking the first step on that big project, admitting we're wrong, or asking for help when we struggle. One small victory can lead to another. And another. And then to big ones. We find that the tough conversation didn't kill us, taking the first step didn't maim us, and asking for help didn't trigger us to ignite on fire. The best way to count coup on fear is to confront it and prove it wrong. Over and over.

When we let fear get in the way of our progress, we won't be able to serve anyone. How can we if we've raised a white flag on ourselves? The gritty, no-quit, bare-knuckle attitude that fuels a healthy warrior spirit is a willingness to face the enemy, fear, and kick its ass. When we do that, we usually see that:

- The thing that scared us wasn't as bad or big as we made it out to be.

- We learned something valuable about ourselves.

- We can gain wisdom when we believe there are no mistakes, only learning.

- We can gain confidence for the next thing. And the next.

What Are We Afraid Of?

Most of the fears we face won't be in the form of an armed enemy on the field of combat or a bear trying to eat us. But it sure can feel that way in the moment. In my conversations with thousands of service providers through the years, I've seen two fears come up time and time again: the fear of failure—falling short in our work, making mistakes, or not being able to deliver on our commitments—and fear of the impending judgment that follows, otherwise known as criticism. Unaddressed, these can lead us to become paralyzed and stagnant, too afraid to act.

The fear of failing to deliver, of stumbling in public, of making a bad call or mistake can shut us down completely as we wait for the perfect moment, the perfect plan, and the perfect resources that will ensure our success. But they never show up. Often in our wait for perfection, the moment we can take action without risk, time passes—and so does the opportunity to make an impact. Those who dedicate their lives to serving others are often eager to please and if that fails, sometimes shame, guilt, and inadequacy are triggered in the void. Instead of seeing a mistake as just a mistake, we can internalize the shortcoming and label ourselves as the mistake.

Not everything you do is going to succeed and not everything you do is going to fail. We're playing the odds here, but the more we face our fear of failure, the more experience we gain, the stronger our courage gets, and the less likely we are to fail. See how that works? Besides, it's usually not the failure we fear most, but the pain of judgment and criticism, from ourselves and others, that always comes spilling in when things don't work out.

Criticism and judgment can leave us feeling alone, cast away, and unworthy. But remember, even the greatest warriors faced the same fears.

Crazy Horse is my hero, and so much better than what we see in superhero movies—Crazy Horse was real. He was the war leader for Sitting Bull, the brilliant tactician at several successful Lakota engagements against the U.S. Army climaxing in the Battle of Little Big Horn, and the fearsome warrior who struck terror in the hearts of brave men who faced him in battle. Crazy Horse was a dedicated warrior for his people, the last Lakota leader to surrender to the U.S. Army. That is what he is remembered for. But when he was young, he was poor, often dirty or disheveled, and a quiet outcast. He was teased mercilessly for having lighter-complected skin and lighter-colored hair and for being smaller and skinnier than the other kids his age. He was a strange boy who grew up to be a strange man, though beloved and revered by his people for his courage, commitment, and character. Yes, Crazy Horse was an iconic warrior. But by today's standards he would have been considered a nerd and he went through the emotional gauntlet that came with that label. Before he ever faced the enemy on the field of battle, he first had to face and overcome the fear of criticism. Let this be a solace when we are judged, criticized, or ridiculed for doing our own thing, going our own way, or just being ourselves. Take heart, we're in great company.

A Lesson from Nature:

The Legend of the Why Trees Lose Their Leaves

Autumn is my favorite season. The beautiful transition of color and cooling weather always stir my spirit. It also reminds me of a story I created for my daughters to explain the falling leaves. Our elders have always said our best lessons can be drawn from nature and the outdoors is our greatest classroom. This story is about a plague that affects us all—criticism. The fear of criticism can be stifling, and it can infect us when we begin to falsely believe that we'll feel better and our insecurities can be remedied by criticizing others.

A long time ago, before human beings, the world was covered in undisturbed forests—but there was no peace. The beautiful broadleaf trees like the elm, oak, and maple never lost their leaves and could change their leaf color from brilliant orange to fire red to bright green whenever they wished. They were robed in glorious leaves and because they felt superior in their beauty, they would ridicule and tease the peaceful pines for their thin and pointed leaves. The broadleaf trees were merciless in their teasing and the pines would cry under the attack, leaking sticky sap tears trailing down their sides. One day, the Creator had seen enough and visited the forests to resolve the conflict.

"For far too long you have attacked and insulted the kindly pine trees of this forest," the Creator admonished. "Now you will suffer the consequences of your arrogance and cruelty." The peaceful pines sat quietly as the broadleaf trees cried out in protest.

"This isn't fair," a stand of majestic oaks argued. "We are far more beautiful than the pines with their ugly, pointy leaves. See how our leaves dance and sway? See how we can change colors whenever we please?" All the broadleaf trees let their leaves dance on the wind and began showing off their colors and thoroughly impressing themselves. In that moment, all the broadleaf trees began to lose their leaves. "What's happening to us?" they all cried out in panic.

Through their lamenting, the Creator announced, "From now on, each autumn your leaves will fall like this to remind you that through criticism of others, you gain nothing—you only lose part of yourself. You will be cold and humble throughout the winter and if you are kind to the pines, you will be given your leaves back in spring. The pines will keep their leaves all year long." The broadleaf trees bowed their branches in shame.

Now, each fall, the broadleaf trees again try to impress the Creator and reverse their fate but only show their pride and vanity. In that moment, their leaves begin to fall, and the cycle is repeated. Throughout the winter, whenever you hear the naked branches squeak together in the wind, this is the sound of the "fallen" trees humbly asking forgiveness for their behavior, so their leaves return in the spring.

Cultivating Courage

We don't have to eliminate fear to take action, but we're much more likely to do so when we cultivate courage in our lives.

How do we do that?

BE A WARRIOR, NOT A WORRIER

When we're able to keep fear in check with our courage, we're able to stay effective in our warrior role. If we let fear overtake us, we slide into the ineffective "worrier" role. When faced with a seemingly impossible task, remember that you don't have to do everything at once. Taking even the smallest action, again and again, goes a long way toward cultivating our courage, and is the difference between creating a warrior and a worrier. Worriers see an obstacle and think, "There's nothing that can be done." So they lament, complain, catastrophize, and end up feeling like victims. They lose the battle before they begin the fight. Warriors, on the other hand, take action, stay solution-oriented by creating a plan of attack, and change tactics as needed. If we face our fear but refuse to take action, worry tends to rush into the void of that gap and create paralysis. Instead, you have to touch the enemy and count coup on fear. Act.

Going through four years of struggle at the U.S. Air Force Academy, I learned that when things get hard, you have to take it a day at a time—but you have to keep pushing. When things get *really* hard, take it one hour at a time—but keep grinding. When we do that, we can make it through anything. Whatever you do, don't quit. When we quit once, the next time is so much more tempting. And easier. As Dory says in the movie *Finding Nemo*, "just keep swimming."

Warriors	Worriers
Action-oriented	Complaint-prone
Willing to risk	Stuck in fear
Focused on solutions	Focused on the problem
Say *"the sky's the limit"* and *"let's get the job done"*	Say *"the sky's falling"* and *"let's find an easier job to do"*

MAKE PAIN YOUR FRENEMY

We all experience pain. It's a natural part of life. Some people have experienced unbelievable amounts of pain and come through stronger, wiser, and more determined than ever. They wrestle it into submission and make it their frenemy (part friend, part enemy) and experience growth. Others ignore, run away from, inflate, or dump off their pain onto others, fostering bitterness in their lives. In turn, they become controlled by their pain.

Pain can be beneficial or detrimental, depending on how we handle it and what we tell ourselves about it. When we push ourselves out of our comfort zone to grow, when we practice self-discipline, when we do hard work and are willing to suffer some to make progress, we experience pain with purpose. Many of our traditional ceremonies incorporated pain and suffering to trigger spiritual growth and prepare warriors for their challenges. Exposure to this kind of pain increases our tolerance so it doesn't slow or stop us when it appears again.

But there is also pain without purpose. This happens when we shift from the natural, normal pain experienced in growth and into an ongoing loop of regret, guilt, or shame. This is not productive use of pain. This is a recipe to stay stuck in "the suck."

Pain can be a teacher, a guide, an internal alarm system— or it can become a destroyer of confidence, an obstacle to progress, or a catalyst to bitterness. How we choose to handle our pain is what makes us who we are and can be improved with small, intentional steps that start with facing it, exploring it, and questioning its purpose and place. Ask yourself, "What story am I telling myself about the pain I'm experiencing?" Are you telling yourself a story of pity and defeat, or are you reveling in a victorious narrative that reminds you that this is part of our struggle to learn, improve, and grow? The answer determines our results.

Pain without purpose is *truly* pain. Pain *with* a purpose is process.

One of the most important choices regarding pain is choosing not to turn away from it before we understand why it has appeared and where it's coming from. When we make it a habit to run from pain, which is tempting, that fosters willful ignorance and keeps us from understanding it. Instead, embrace your pain and hug it close until you choke it out—and can replace it with something else, like clarity, understanding, or acceptance. The ones who learn to *deal with* their pain effectively become successful. The ones who learn to *embrace* their pain into submission become unstoppable. I've known pain and so have you. And it will come again. What will you do with yours?

DUMP THE THREE ENEMIES THAT LEAVE US
FEELING RAW: REGRET, ANGER, AND WORRY

There are a few elements in particular that can stifle our ability to cultivate courage, drawing our focus away from what we *can* do in the moment to ruminating on unproductive thoughts. Regret is a waste of time because we can't change the past. Learn any relevant lessons and move on. Anger is a volatile force that can be used for good in the short term only, if it's handled carefully and harnessed properly. But anger can also become draining and cause health issues when used as a long-term fuel source. Let things go, forgive, and learn how to pick your battles wisely. Worry is a waste of time and energy—most of what we worry about never happens anyway. These three add little to no benefit in the cultivation of courage and can cause serious harm to you and others.

HONE YOUR WAR CRY

In Native tradition, a war cry was typically a full-throated scream accompanied by wild gesticulations. Our warriors cried out their war cry before battling the enemy for two important reasons. The first was to scare the shit out of the enemy, leaving them in a trembling puddle, and to win the fight psychologically before it even began. The second was to inspire themselves with a burst of energetic courage to face the challenge ahead. One of the best war cries ever is from our brothers and sisters the Maori, Native people of New Zealand. They do the haka, a dancing chant performed by warriors, both men and women, to intimidate and challenge enemies. It culminates with the tongue sticking out, which means: "We're not just going to defeat you . . . we're going to eat you." Wow, now *that* is a war cry that would melt any enemy.

As warriors, we should practice our war cry often to cultivate courage. Sometimes our war cry is pathetic. When facing challenges, if our internal dialogue is defeatist or negative ("Oh no, here we go again," or "How on earth is this going to

work?" or "This seems too hard already"), then the poor results we get should come as no surprise. You can't get positive
outcomes with negative mindsets. You need a better war cry.

Create a war cry that boosts your strength, resolve, and
determination and is a direct feed to your warrior spirit. Your
war cry doesn't have to be shouted at full volume, and wild
gesticulations aren't necessary. A war cry can be a mantra,
prayer, quote, activity, or even something you touch, hold, or
wear. It should be something personal and meaningful that
you can go to time after time like a touchstone, to provide a
dose of strength and confidence to bring out your best when
you need it most.

Remember, courage is fostered and practiced, it is not automatic. And if you do decide to do your war cry at full volume, make sure your coworkers or neighbors aren't around.
You may scare the shit out of *them*.

ACKNOWLEDGE YOUR COURAGEOUS MOMENTS

We can build a memory bank of strength, a strong reminder of
our bravery, when we acknowledge the times where we have
exercised courage. So often we focus on where we got scared,
came up short, or stumbled instead of giving ourselves
credit for all the countless moments of bravery we've shown.
Acknowledging your courageous moments creates a reser-
voir of reminders, good memories, and confidence that you've
been here before and can face whatever is ahead of you. After all, whatever challenge you may be facing, personally or

professionally, I bet money you've been through something just as tough—or worse—and you're still here doing your thing. Lean on that truth. Grow that memory bank on purpose. It'll serve you well on the journey ahead.

And if you don't feel courageous, borrow courage from your peers and teammates.

Shane Coyne resembles a classic action hero, stocky, with short-cropped blond hair, an effervescent personality, and a cherubic face that belies the heart of a warrior. He's a retired military officer who served in Iraq and has also been a wild-lands firefighter for over twenty years, fighting monster blazes like the Waldo Canyon Fire and the Black Forest Fire in the Colorado Springs area. When he talks on the subject, he is quick to point out how progressive growth happens through a step-by-step climb up the courage ladder. Small victories over time often lead to bigger ones.

Shane's first fire was at a military training area where .50-caliber ordnance was igniting and going off! Of course he was worried, but the calm, collected, and professional behavior of the more experienced firefighters was helpful in alleviating his own fears. He called it "borrowed courage," which helped develop his own. This experience and others led to his ability to cover hundreds of miles in high-stress convoys through Iraq while a member of the military during the war. In turn, that experience enabled him to eventually face the Waldo Canyon Fire, referred to by firefighters as "the beast," which killed two people and consumed 346 homes.

For Shane, it seemed like all his training and previous

experiences had prepared him for this moment. His team showed up to see blocks of neighborhoods on fire and felt overwhelmed but rallied when one of their leaders said, "Don't focus on the losses. Focus on the fight." The Waldo Canyon Fire was deeply personal because it was happening in their own backyard, and the accountability to their friends and neighbors was palpable. The firefighters knew no more reserves were coming, and Shane harkened back to what he told young firefighters when they joined the teams: "Train relentlessly and constantly, so when that moment comes, you're ready and worthy of the task at hand. You don't know when it'll be or what it'll look like, but it will come." For Shane, the time had arrived, and he was prepared to count coup on his fear. They worked tirelessly for thirty-eight hours straight. He said, "This is our town, we're not going to quit. No one is coming to save us. We have to do this." And they did.

Like our traditional warriors, Shane considers the responsibility of service to be both an honor and an obligation. He told me, "You know you've got a skill set and can do something about it, you've got the skill set to be the person in that moment to answer the call and go in there and make a difference, face danger and serve people. Who else is going to go?" Shane wholeheartedly believes training is a key factor in developing courage because it allows familiarity with fear and removes some of the mystery and anxiety. He said, "This allows us to face fear and still be able to operate because we remain an asset and not a liability." Here's a quote he shares with his teams before the fire season starts each year:

We are entering a busy operational period soon, but we are professionals, and professionals regardless of circumstances continue to show up, show up consistently, train relentlessly, and prepare for whatever comes next. Let's always be the professionals we claim to be and know we want to be for each other and the citizens we serve.

KNOW WHEN TO ASK FOR HELP

Remember, exercising courage isn't about swimming with sharks or bungee jumping, it's about confronting challenges head-on, asking for help, being vulnerable with someone you love, and taking that next step forward when we're struggling.

Alex was one of my lieutenants when I was a captain in the Air Force. He was a focused and disciplined officer and a talented athlete (he was an alternate in the 2000 Olympics in Sydney for the U.S. tae kwon do team), and he had the heart and spirit of a warrior. When 9/11 happened, Alex rushed to get into the pipeline for Air Force Special Operations. The timeline was too long, so he lobbied the U.S. Army, which took him into the Special Forces training pipeline right away.

One day while on a patrol mission in Iraq—the worst of all bad days, as Alex describes it—his unit was ambushed. Right before it happened, Alex sensed things were about to go wrong. He said a quiet prayer, slowed his breathing, unbuckled his seat belt, and checked gear and weapons. He then made the radio check-ins and gave commands to his crew to establish a battle position. After that, he told me, the scenario became a "grainy slide projector image" set to a soundtrack of gunfire, explosions, yelling, the taste of dust, and the smell of burnt gunpowder. It was a living nightmare but one he navigated successfully due to his training and experience.

Alex was awarded the Bronze Star for heroic service in combat, but what he experienced next would take all the courage he had.

Alex returned to his family a different man, expressing all the signs of PTSD but not understanding his rage, erratic behavior, and depression. His behavior was a cry for help that no one, not even Alex, recognized. My friend was on a path of self-destruction and became his own worst enemy. And no matter how much they loved him, his family couldn't understand what he'd experienced. Looking every part the elite, hardened soldier he'd been—six-one, bulked out at 250 pounds, covered in tattoos, and wearing a full beard—he presented a scary figure to his loved ones when he was out of control, which was often.

The breaking point, and point of salvation, happened after a rage erupted and his small daughter bravely stood in front of him and screamed, "I hate you."

Alex told me, "I walked out of the house, barefoot in the snow, hands bleeding from punching walls, to a gas station pay phone that was miles from my house. There, I called the help line for the final time in my life and submitted to my flawed humanity, that this was never who I was meant to become." His daughter's courage inspired his own, and he saw how out of alignment his warrior role had become. He'd called the National Suicide Prevention Lifeline many times before, but he said without any real correction, it was like "putting a Band-Aid on a broken bone." In this painful rock-bottom moment, and with his daughter's example, Alex finally felt the leverage to change. Regarding vulnerability or the need to ask for help, he said he was scared to own it and programmed to be embarrassed to even be experiencing it. He called his resistance to asking for help "humiliated by humility" and described it as the "ultimate mental and emotional battlefield no soldier ever really leaves." He said, "Until I recognized being a warrior is more important than being a soldier, I never really thought about it."

Of course, Alex is heroic for what he did in combat. He showed true courage on the worst day of his military experience. But he showed even greater courage when he finally opened up publicly about his personal struggles with PTSD and how it had affected his life and family. His story illustrates that even after experiencing the horrors of hardened combat, the fears of admitting we need help, being vulnerable, and sharing our story can be as scary as anything we face.

Alex says, "I asked for help. I still ask for help. I will ask for help. Warriors aren't individual operators; they're contributing parts to a more important tribe." He faced his fears with courage and counted coup on them. He reminds us that the greatest battlefield we ever face is the one within us. Alex still struggles at times, but he is healthy, happy, and living his best life, both personally and professionally, with his family in Colorado. His example inspires me still and I got goose bumps even sharing his story. Alex is my hero.

_'_

When we face our fears again and again, just like the Plains tribes counted coup on their enemies, we'll find that over time we've built up reservoirs of courage that can sustain us over the long run. It isn't easy, and it requires us to do a lot of hard things, like face down our own ego, embrace our vulnerability—even ask for help at times. But if we want to be warriors, not worriers, in our roles, we can't be afraid to embrace what scares us.

5

Attack Again and Again

Overcoming the Impossible

I felt the blood drain from my face as I read the first article that came up in my Google search: "Question: Who hikes the Kalalau Trail? Answer: Dumb and dumber." I was with one of my best friends, Aaron Lawson, who was retiring from the Air Force, where he had been in Special Operations as a combat controller (aka badass). To celebrate the end of an era, he'd invited his friends to do something "epic." I should've known to be concerned when I was the only one who answered the call.

The Kalalau Trail is one of the most dangerous hikes in the world. It goes across the north coast of Kauai and is composed of packed clay, slick mud, and crumbly volcanic rock pathways that steeply go up and down for over eleven miles.

The other articles that came up on my Google search high-lighted the deaths and accidents that had resulted in the trail being dubbed the "Kalalua Death Trail."

Aaron and I started the hike with full packs and high spir-its. The gnawing doubt lingered but was kept at bay as we made progress through the jungle. But as the day went on, the eleven-mile trail got progressively worse, becoming grueling and then terrifying when we traversed a narrow half-mile path of crumbly lava rock that was barely wide enough for one person. Hundreds of feet below us were jagged rocks and the foaming ocean.

Nine hours later we limped into the campsite as the sun was going down. My legs trembled like a newborn colt, and I almost fell into the camp stove from exhaustion. I started having shock diarrhea like runners do after a marathon. This was not "epic." This sucked.

We were in an isolated tropical paradise, but I couldn't have been more miserable. I was trying to recover between bouts of continued diarrhea as Aaron played in the ocean with a group of naked hippies who hung out in this remote area. I was pumping water through filtration from the only good water source, a pool formed by a beautiful waterfall. Unfortunately, the pool also contained dozens of giant toads mating and the water was filled with ribbons of gelatinous eggs that kept clogging the water filter. Squatted down, I looked up to see a man's privates at eye level. He was one of the group of hippies, all naked as jaybirds coming to get their water too. They were friendly and invited us to a pot-fueled drum party that I had no interest in attending.

Toads. Naked hippies. Diarrhea. Epic.

I finally had a heart-to-heart with Aaron. I told him I was upset and worried about the trek back, but also because I couldn't get hydrated with the frequent diarrhea. Luckily, he had an awesome first aid kit and antidiarrheal meds. He told me he was worried too, that this was much tougher than he'd thought it would be. He said that when those in his profession were about to do a dangerous mission, it was paramount to put all thoughts of home, family, being somewhere else, etc. out of mind and focus on only what needed to be done. He broke open the small flask of whiskey he had in his med kit and we each took sips. We agreed the only thing we needed to focus on was walking out of here in the morning.

It was a fitful night under the stars. I finally was hydrated, but was so anxious, I hardly ate anything at dinner. I lay in the tent awake, dreading the hike back. In the morning, we broke camp and packed up before sunrise and as soon as we had light, we started moving out. The path immediately got steep, traversing up red clay mounds, and we were already sweating as we crossed the first river. I leapt across the river one large rock at a time. The first. The second. And as I jumped to the riverbank, my foot slammed into a rock ledge and I heard a loud "pop!" We were out here with no rangers, no communication, no rescue options. I was too scared to admit I was injured when Aaron yelled out, "Dude, you all right?" My immediate response was, "I'm good!" I wasn't good.

The next ten miles and ten hours were pure agony. Not only was the hike just as grueling, but I was doing it on few calories, a compromised body that hadn't recovered, and now a broken foot and big toe. I was pissed off, scared, exhausted, and injured. Plus, the knowledge of the upcoming lava cliffs added terror. I winced with each step and had tears in my eyes at several points but just kept putting one foot in front of the other, over and over again. Despite the exhaustion, the shooting pain that turned to a constant throb, one foot in front of the other. With each lightning bolt of pain from my foot, I started to embrace the fact that I was still moving, still alive, and let the frustration fuel my progress. My emotions were all over the place, but I stayed focused on putting one foot in front of the other. The only way we were getting out of here was to walk out.

And we did. After those ten hours of hiking out, we met Aaron's uncle Joel, who greeted us as we emerged from the jungle with a can of ice-cold coconut water. It was the best thing I ever tasted.

There Is No Substitute for Action

There will be times when you face a seemingly insurmountable task that might hurt or even scare the hell out of you. You might be faced with having to fire an employee, lead a complex project, or deal with a divorce or cancer diagnosis. To get through them, you might be tempted to look for the poetic or pretty solution, but most of the time, the solution is just to gut it out until it's done. It might hurt, be scary and uncomfortable, but that lasts only until it's over. When things suck so bad, if you just keeping taking one step after excruciating step, you can figuratively walk yourself right out of hell and save yourself in the process.

Our tribal warriors of the past highlight great examples of the power of consistent action, specifically in how they were innovative experts in guerrilla warfare. In battle, they would attack aggressively, withdraw, regroup, and then attack again until they defeated their enemies. With that relentless dynamic, our Native warriors were able to defend against, or defeat, larger and better-equipped enemies. Opponents became demoralized in battle when they realized about our warriors, "They just keep coming back over and over and from different directions. They won't quit!" In fact, the ragtag and ill-equipped Continental Army of the early United States also relied on this guerrilla fighting technique, learned from Indigenous warriors, to defeat Great Britain, the mightiest nation in the world at the time.

No matter how good your excuse for not taking on a challenge, there is no substitute for action. Like with cultivating courage, simply taking the first step toward a goal, whether it's starting a project or getting back in shape, pops the bubble of tension, doubt, and worry that grows in its absence.

Action also pops the bubble of perfection. How often do

we delay and wait for the perfect moment, the perfect set of circumstances or resources, before we decide to act? Those perfect conditions seldom appear, and we stay stuck in a holding pattern. When we take a first step forward, we see that things aren't so scary and that we can do this. Besides, creating something beautiful or successful is never about creating something perfect. The Navajo Tribe has a tradition that reminds us of this. When Navajo weavers create one of their famous beautiful rugs or blankets, they purposefully stitch a flaw in the rug to embrace imperfection. The lesson here is to embrace your quirks and just do the work.

Unfortunately, we live in a world where we're taught from a young age that wishing for something can make it come true without us having to work for it. We have wishing wells that suckered us out of pocket change as kids. As adults, we have lottery tickets. Wishing gets us off the hook of work and sets us up for frustration and disappointment. I've heard that the best way to predict our future is to create it. We do that through work. Work is about action, exercising our will; it's the quintessence of empowerment. Instead of saying "I wish for," a better, more empowering mantra is "I work for."

I believe in prayer, though the Creator's plans don't always match ours.

I believe in hope, but not as a strategy for growth, progress, or change.

I believe wishing is for suckers and fairy tales.

I believe in work. Work doesn't sit back and wait for things to happen, it *makes* them happen.

And as my friend and four-time Olympian Ruben Gonzalez says in his book *The Courage to Succeed*, "Pray like it's in God's hands. Work like it's in ours."

One of my favorite examples of the transformative power of taking consistent action is Dr. Katherine Campbell (Winnebago). Kat is a trailblazer and passionate leader in education and works as a monitor and advocate for Tribal Colleges and Universities (TCUs) for the Bureau of Indian Education. Kat has lived her life as a series of relentless steps in a focused effort, refusing to quit or change directions. She understands the value of consistent, committed action because her journey has been a living embodiment of those principles.

She says, "The warrior spirit comes through when you remember that you fight for others. One of my spiritual advisers told me, when you are doing the work you should, help will always show up. I had gone to school with one purpose in mind: to go home and help my people."

Kat grew up with disruption, racism, and poverty. She flunked the second grade because the bus across town was always late. Moving to the Rosebud Reservation in the fifth grade, she found the school didn't have a library, only a little truck that brought some books every two weeks. Kat encountered a teacher who had a vast collection and Kat excitedly asked if she could read some. The teacher was shocked that Kat had no books at home and loaded her up. That small action sparked Kat's fascination with learning and the transformative power of education.

Kat says, "When I was in seventh grade, I had a language

arts teacher who would flip young Native boys' braids and ask them why they didn't cut their hair because it was so dirty. I saw how those boys would literally curl up under her words and I felt so angry and powerless. When I was in high school, I was looking at the bulletin boards the teacher had put up. They were all white. I wondered why there wasn't anyone like me in the pictures at the front of the room." Those were the seeds planted in her mind that fueled her fight to become a teacher and she leveraged them now.

She became the first generation in her family to graduate from college. I met her while she was teaching on the Winnebago Reservation. I was a young Air Force lieutenant recruiting for the U.S. Air Force Academy and was there for school visits. Her passion for her path was obvious and we've been friends ever since, sharing our hopes and dreams of how we wanted to impact our Native communities. And the world.

It didn't surprise me that a few years afterward, she continued her climb to develop so she could fulfill that warrior role and serve tribal communities in a wider and deeper way. She went back to school to get her master's degree and threw herself into her work, letting her original purpose fuel her forward motion. Even as a single mom working as a graduate assistant and taking a full course load, she graduated in a year. With a 4.0. She went on to a full fellowship and struggled mightily through statistics, learning computer skills, and missing time with her kids; she developed stress eczema. But she left that program with PhD in hand.

Without her ability to consistently face the seemingly impossible, Kat acknowledges that she never would have made it. She stayed focused on her goals, gathered and rallied support from mentors and role models, and paid attention to what she needed—and then found a way to provide it. All this allowed her to keep putting one foot in front of the other, again and again, taking consistent action and continuing to move forward. Kat continues to be an enthusiastic evangelist at a national level for transforming Indian education to better serve Native students and communities.

Discipline: The One Thing We Can Control

We don't control much in this world beyond what we think, say, and do. But our ability to execute focused, consistent action is something we *can* control, and we can see great results when we do so.

Discipline gets a bad rap because more often than not, we've experienced it as something done *to* us, and frequently in a punitive or harsh manner. But our talents and abilities go to waste if we can't harness them through the power of self-discipline. After all, a fireplace can offer a warming glow. But if you harness and magnify that fire the right way, you can launch a rocket into outer space.

Discipline is doing what we need to do, when we need to do it, *even when we don't feel like it.* Another way to remember it is "work before play" or "dinner before dessert." Discipline gives us structure and stability. When we practice doing a *few things* each day toward the direction of goals, we prevent the feeling of overwhelm that comes with trying to do *everything* in one day. And when we follow this dynamic, there is no limit to how good we can become at what we do and who we are. We become our own self-fulfilling prophecy of excellence.

In the same way, our tribal warrior traditions toughened the body and disciplined the mind through practices such as fasting, chipping away ice to swim, exposure to the elements, or the rigors of stickball and ceremonies such as the vision quest. No one *made* our warriors do it. They *chose* to do it, because they knew it made them stronger, tougher, and more resilient and successful in their role.

Ask yourself, how are you practicing discipline daily to develop more of yourself? What tasks could you be better at attacking each day?

The Magic of Momentum

In our own lives and careers, the most effective way to leverage action is by doing it consistently. And that requires self-discipline. Our warriors didn't practice shooting a bow and arrow once and say they were a good hunter, just as going to the gym once doesn't make us fit. Self-discipline to act consistently is how habits are created, battles are won, marathons are run, societies and systems change, and strength is developed. Once you see results from your actions, you'll find it easier to keep striving. That's the power of momentum at work. As my friend and mentor Mark LeBlanc says, "Success is not determined by results, but by your momentum. Your momentum is determined by how you feel. How we feel is determined by the consistent, daily application of the best we have within us."

Taking consistent, focused action in the right direction creates a momentum that leads us to higher and bolder actions. We start to feel confidence when we see results. This creates a self-fulfilling dynamic that pushes us even higher. This is where life and career really get exciting, and we start overcoming the obstacles that held us back. Or going right through them. This is where we truly grow beyond our current capacity. Sometimes, that next bold action may seem like more than we can do; but the momentum fizzles, doubt appears, and results cease when we stop acting. We know what is possible only when we take that next bold leap of faith and grow our wings on the way down.

Momentum is achieved only through action, not intention. The seemingly small, consistent acts we make create that magical energy of momentum. Momentum creates confidence, courage, results, and excitement, which add major horsepower to our warrior spirit. Momentum is how boats get up on plane and how the brown basilisk, also known as the Jesus Christ lizard, can literally run on top of the water. It's how kernels become popcorn, through the building up of energy and heat. On the other hand, hesitation creates doubt, fear, no results, and boredom. If we shut off the microwave in frustration at the two-minute mark due to lack of progress, we wouldn't see all the explosive popping in the third minute and get to enjoy the popcorn at the end of it. In the same way, the longer you stay at your task and continue putting one foot in front of the other, the easier it gets to keep going. This is how you can build a business, write a book, get in shape, restore a car or house, or create a life and career you can be proud of.

Remember, your success is never about doing *everything* in *one* day, it's about doing something *every* day—that will eventually get you wherever you want to go. The results may take time, but they will appear.

We've all heard that an overnight success takes twenty years. This is a reminder to understand and appreciate all the effort that led to that moment. All the work, the sacrifices, the grinding through the doubt and fear—all get overlooked by the brightness of the victory. When we lived in Colorado, I was getting into my car when I noticed the entire slab of the concrete driveway was cleaved in half! Now, it wasn't like that the day before, so it seemed to happen overnight. But the truth is that over years of heat, cold, wet, dry, contraction, expansion, the concrete was being broken even though I couldn't see it. The crack was the last, most visible proof of the process, that's all.

My friend Dr. Karen Goodnight (Chickasaw) understands the power and necessity of creating momentum through consistent actions. She has had a long and storied career in education, business, and leadership development, and is now an executive coach, helping other dedicated servants to achieve their own victories. In the early years of her career, she wanted to work with children and studied child development. Her plan was to teach in public school, but her passion, talent, and abilities led to an opportunity to become her tribe's Head Start director.

One step led to another . . . While Karen was there, she learned about development and management of not only children but other employees and parents too. That opened another door, a drive to get involved in leadership development.

One step led to another . . . She got an incredible opportunity to serve her tribe in the enterprise and employee development arena, rising to the highest heights in the organization.

One step led to another . . . and bigger and bolder ones too. Karen's success led her to decide to go out on her own. Through support, guidance, and a heavy use of her warrior spirit, Karen faced her obstacles and fears and leveraged momentum for another success. She now serves on her tribe's legislature. She says, "We all face obstacles that force us to use our courage when facing the possibility of failure, though failing is all part of learning and growing. Tapping into our warrior spirit can provide that extra strength when we need it the most."

Karen believes that there is no substitute for momentum we create through consistent action, saying, "The small, fundamental steps are the most important ones. It takes small steps to start the process. Once you've tackled that, everything else will follow and momentum happens."

You Get What You Focus On

Years ago, around Halloween, I was staying in a hotel for a work event. The TV had only a handful of channels. One of them was AMC and they were having Scream Week, all horror films. Watching flick after flick of ghosts, slashers, and monsters, I became solely focused on . . . fear. Every noise was a ghost. Every shadow was a ghoul. When it was time for my event, I threw a shirt over my head and felt a hand on my back. My blood ran cold. I moved forward and felt the hand slide a few inches. I yelled, jumped forward, and looked back—only to watch a dryer sheet fall lazily to the floor.

A simple truth we learn over and over again is that we get what we focus on. That idea or activity we focus on becomes a lens we see through and starts to guide our thoughts, actions, and results. Our warriors were focused on their role, and everything they did in their activity went through that funnel of focus—what they learned, how they trained, how they cared for their body, mind, and spirit, all revolved around their focus to serve and protect their people as best they could with whatever they had. Our focus leads us by the nose in a direction that our bodies will follow, so we need to stay aware of what we're focused on and what we're trying to do.

How often have we derailed our own process or walked away from opportunities because fear was our focus? Our thoughts turn to catastrophe, magnified out of proportion. And sometimes, it's just a damn dryer sheet.

Other times, we derail our own progress by focusing on too much at once.

THE DANGER OF MULTITASKING

One of the quickest ways to divide and conquer ourselves in our warrior role is to fall prey to the pressure to multitask. Multitasking is doing many things at one time . . . poorly. When we multitask, we are more likely to make mistakes, have difficulty connecting with others, and increase our stress and anxiety. Some people are so proud of this seeming ability that they multitask while they multitask. When you see someone talk on the phone, check email, eat a sandwich, organize files, and give hand signals to the person standing in their doorway, you'll see the chaos in real time. I call it a "seeming" ability because of the way our brains are built. We're able to focus effectively on only one thing at a time. People will argue and say, "Can't be true because I can walk and talk." First thing I always say is "awesome" (and give a thumbs-up). But in all seriousness, what are you focused on while you walk and talk? Are you focused on the spatial orientation of your pelvis to the ground, how high you lift your knees, or where you place each foot? No, of course not. You're focused on the conversation (especially if it's juicy!).

I learned painfully as a kid that riding a bike while playing dodgeball or climbing a tree while playing tag was a bad combination. The first ended with a flight over my handlebars, hitting my face on the street, splitting my lip, and putting deep scratches on my new glasses. The second ended with me writhing on the ground while trying to catch my breath after falling fifteen feet out of an oak tree. These same poor results show up in our lives when we're trying to have a high-quality conversation while checking email, working on a project while listening to someone's office squabbles, or trying to do last-minute, nonurgent tasks while lying in bed before sleep. Most things are meant to be done only one at a time. Or sometimes not at all.

-:-

We oftentimes overthink our next actions or wait for perfect timing or the perfect move. And end up making none. We miss out on opportunities, chances to grow and to move forward in our lives and careers. I'm a belted practitioner in Krav Maga, which is Hebrew for "contact combat." It is a practical, off-the-shelf self-defense and fighting system that is one of the most effective in existence. It cherry-picks the best of boxing, jujitsu, wrestling, muay Thai, etc. and even street fighting. The moves in Krav Maga are simple, aggressive, and designed to fight as efficiently and quickly as possible. Another way to describe the moves is that *it doesn't need to be pretty, it just has to work*. The basic moves of punching, hammer fists, and kicks build confidence and lead to more complex ground-fighting skills, and eventually to learning how to take on multiple tar-gets and even disarming opponents with weapons. When faced with an opponent, we use what's available in that moment to win. We don't overthink. We don't question. We just do the next simple move. And then the next. Until we win.

What does all this create, if we attack and then attack again, leverage self-discipline, consistently take right action, avoid multitasking, and take bold actions? What it creates is results! Sometimes, the results we want don't come at the speed we'd like or in the form we'd expect, but it doesn't mean that what we're doing isn't working. Stay the course.

Now, let's delve into a burning question that can lead us to burnout if we can't answer it: "How do I sustain my strength and stay motivated when things get beyond busy and I feel weary, run-down, and depleted?"

6

Keep the Fires Lit

Sustaining Your Strength in the Headwinds

n our Native American cultures, the role of a firekeeper was a sacred and solemn duty. A fire was the beating heart of a village, central to the well-being and happiness of the tribe. It provided health through the sustenance of cooked food, made light in the darkness, gave comfort through warmth, and served as a gathering place for people to share stories and strengthen their bonds. Fire was also the critical element in most sacred ceremonies. If it went out, the ceremony could be ruined. A firekeeper's job was to keep it burning through all conditions.

In our own lives and careers, we have a fire inside us. Our warrior spirit is an internal energy that fuels our drive, willingness to learn and serve, and commitment to excellence.

Just like the village fire, we must tend that fire carefully and intentionally, or it can burn down to an ember—or even go out.

Our warriors maintained their fire by remembering that their role had deep personal and spiritual meaning. They knew they were fulfilling a sacred duty, an ultimate expression of the expectation of a committed tribal member. They were also in environments that constantly reminded them of their role, encouraged them in it, and rewarded them for it. Being a warrior could be an honorable, deeply fulfilling, and even joyful experience. But it was also dangerous, hard, and sometimes deadly. So the motivation was not automatic. It was fostered. It was created purposefully.

Could you imagine an unmotivated warrior? He crawls out of the lodge in midafternoon with disheveled hair, rubbing his eyes, looking around bewildered while yawning, and lazily asks, "What do I have to do today?" Or worse, a warrior who refuses to come out of the lodge. He would not have achieved excellence, enabled victory, or inspired confidence in the people in his tribe who were depending on him. Yet many of us who occupy very important positions in healthcare, education, community building, government, and benevolent businesses are operating in the same lackluster way. And there's a reason for it.

We all start with a bright, burning fire in our hearts when we begin our endeavors to serve others well. You feel inspired in your role; it's a new thing and it excites you. You learn your new responsibilities as quickly as you can and your learning curve is vertical. Eventually, you get into a rhythm once you start understanding what's expected of you and how you can deliver it, and you begin to get a feel for the schedule, the personalities of coworkers and clients, and how the days unfold. Then that rhythm starts to feel like routine, where you fully know what's expected of you. You deliver consistently, but the schedule and the personalities are starting to get old and the days longer. Eventually, you stop taking breaks, asking for or accepting help, organizing, and prioritizing; self-care goes out the window; and you become overwhelmed. As time goes on, you fall into a rut. Now the role you were once excited about is all . . . blah. You're no longer fighting to make a difference, you're just fighting to make it to the weekend. What happened?

You got tricked into believing the big lie: If you've chosen the right path, motivation will always be there automatically. But if you take that dynamic for granted, it doesn't matter how important your work may be or how dedicated you are to it. That fire can burn down to an ember. Or even go out.

The sure way to stay stuck in "off mode" is to start beating yourself up over your newly emerged lack of commitment. You might be asking yourself, "What is wrong with me? Why don't I care anymore or as much as I used to? I got into this to help people. Maybe I'm not the person I thought I was (or hoped I was)." But burnout can happen to any of us if we don't keep ourselves motivated on purpose, with purpose and consistency. Can you imagine an elder barking at a firekeeper who let the fire go out and the firekeeper says, "Aw, my bad. I put a log on it last week. I thought it'd be enough. I thought it'd last." It isn't. It doesn't. We must keep feeding our fires.

The reality is, we are the only ones who can create and maintain our fires. Not our friends, employer, or supervisor. Motivation is not automatic. After all, do we live in a positive or negative world? Of course, that's a loaded question and we know that our perspective and attitude shape our reality. But what can't be argued is that there is much negativity in the world. We don't have to look far to find it, we just have to turn on the news or have a conversation at the grocery store. If we're in that type of world every day, why would we think doing something "motivational" every once in a while is good enough? It's not even close.

Our warrior spirit needs what all living things need: continual feeding. We need to be vigilant in the way we manage our motivation. Without it, we stop fighting so hard and don't care as much. And if that dynamic continues, we face burnout and experience the emotional bottom of the barrel regarding serving others, which is apathy. Apathy is where we give up and no longer care at all.

The Right Kind of Motivation

Motivation is simply a reason to do something and the willingness to do it. That's it. If a flood started filling your home with water, you'd be motivated to leave as soon as possible.

The more compelling the reason we have to do something, the more motivated we are to do it. Motivation is a key component in the warrior spirit. It's the rocket fuel that makes it go.

But it's important we create the right kind of motivation. Though there are many types of motivation, according to behavioral scientists, I think there are two basic flavors and we've all tasted both: motivation by fear and motivation by joy.

FEAR COSTS US

Years ago, I traveled to Australia when I was in the military and took some leave to dive on the Great Barrier Reef with one of my best friends, Troy Harting. We were like kids in a candy store, pointing out the vibrant-colored coral and fish through excited smiles and bubbles. Suddenly, Troy's hand hit my face mask and knocked it crooked. I looked at him annoyed and saw he was pointing at a shark in our vicinity—and it was swimming closer to me! What do experts say to do when near a shark? Stay calm and don't make sudden movements.

Yeah, right. We took off, and I swear we could've been competitive for Olympic tryouts if we'd been timed.

Does motivation by fear work? Yes, it can. But it's the worst form of motivation. Motivation by fear requires us to constantly threaten ourselves with endless scenarios of bad outcomes. The problem with motivating ourselves with a stick is that we must keep getting a bigger stick, and eventually motivation by fear doesn't work anymore. It just beats us down, jacks up our anxiety, and leads us to burnout.

JOY SUSTAINS US

On the other hand, motivation by joy is a much deeper pool to draw from, nicer to experience, and, more importantly, sustainable. It's tapped when we frequently remind ourselves of what is going right, what is possible, why it matters, and how cool we are with all our capabilities, skills, and power.

As I mentioned earlier, our warriors were always motivated because their role had deep, personal, and spiritual meaning to them. In the same way, to sustain our motivation in what we do, our work must matter to us more than it does to anyone else. Our work must have meaning that goes beyond our job description, what our boss says it is, or what it may mean to other people. The real meaning behind our work is what *we* say it is.

Your meaning can be any combination of reasons, whether it's a focus on accountability, a passionate mission, teaching a new generation of changemakers, protecting your community, helping people whose shoes you've been in, or anything else that drives us to do what we do. But the meaning *matters*, and it's up to us to define it. When we infuse our roles with meaning, we can rise in motivation to face the challenges ahead with our warrior spirit intact. Without meaning, it's hard to get out of the car once we get to work.

Years ago, I was a presenter at the annual National Character and Leadership Symposium hosted by the U.S. Air Force Academy. I ran into a young, eager airman who was a refueler for C-17 cargo aircraft. He'd won a service award at his base for his excellence on the job. Now, putting fuel in an aircraft may not seem all that, but the way this guy described his role made me want to do it too! He said, "When I'm out there refueling those aircraft, whether it's blazing hot, freezing cold, or the rain is coming down sideways, I remember why I'm there. I know that these birds are going to bring equipment, medical supplies, packages from home, and all sorts of things our men and women in harm's way need." He smiled. "I also know when they come back, they'll be bringing Americans home to their families." He was pure purpose and I got fired up listening to him. He finally said, "That's my focus. Always. Some people out there are just pumping gas."

Now, who would you want fueling up your aircraft? I'd want that guy ten out of ten times! Same job, two different people, two completely different mindsets. Who gave his work meaning? He did. And it made all the difference in the way he felt about what he did and the way he did it each day.

How to Fuel Your Fire

So, if we understand better what motivation is, why it matters, and how we create it, the real question is: How do you maintain motivation in the face of setbacks, struggles, and overwhelm?

TAP INTO YOUR TRIBE

When we stay engaged with and connected to our tribe, our network, we strengthen our motivation when we see what's possible and feed our curiosity. We're updating our mental files as to what's going on and opportunities available, as well as who and what might be able to help us solve our challenges. We lose track of what's happening around us, and often *to* us, if we don't keep our heads up and maintain situational awareness. Staying connected to our peers and network keeps us constantly "nudged" in the right direction, like a guided missile flying toward a target. Little microcorrections keep us on course, as do our conversations, and encouragement and ideas we get from our tribe.

I've been blown away over the years by how many times I've found a quick solution to a problem or a resource I needed just by talking to my friends and colleagues. The world is constantly adding new paths and possibilities that we can leverage if we stay engaged. If you're trying to get to the other side of a twenty-foot wall, would you rather try to knock it down or simply ask the person standing next to you if you could borrow their ladder?

KEEP THE CHALLENGES IN PERSPECTIVE

We all tend to catastrophize because our brains developed from the start to look for problems and threats (e.g., knowing that bears can eat us, fire can burn us, water can drown us, and enemy tribes could harm us). Now, add this tendency to jump to conclusions to our incredible imaginations and you've got a recipe for quickly blowing things out of proportion.

When, not if, you experience setbacks, take a moment to ask yourself, "Is this a showstopper or just a speed bump?" and "Am I making this a bigger deal than it is?" Talk it out with a friend; journal about it. It takes discipline and a reality check to keep our challenges in perspective and realize each is just another problem to solve, that's all, instead of an unmitigated crisis. The goal in those moments is to *clarify, not magnify* what is really happening and put it into context so we can get back to moving forward.

REMEMBER YOUR PAST VICTORIES

It's a shame that so often we forget all the work we've done to get to where we are—and do what we're capable of—today, now. Recalling memories of previous successes, where we served with distinction or crushed a project, can bring back those feelings of pride and accomplishment we felt in those moments, and remind us unequivocally that we have skills, abilities, and experiences that can serve us in this new moment of challenge. When we remember what we've been able to do in the past, we can boost our confidence. And remember this again: Whatever you're going through right now, I bet you've been through something just as tough. Or worse. And you're still here doing your thing. Please don't overlook that truth.

GO BACK TO YOUR VALUES
AND FOLLOW YOUR VISION

Our motivation can waver quickly when we forget what we're fighting to create. Go back to your values and vision for a quick hit of motivation. Earlier, we talked about the power of knowing our values and how everything becomes much easier and clearer when we know what to say yes to and what to say no to. Our values feed our vision, and when we remind ourselves of what we're trying to create, we get motivated by the imagery of what could be. When the fear or setbacks show up, it is vital to trust in the plan, not the emotions we feel. Our emotions whisper lies to protect us from disappointment, like "It won't work" or "Who am I to think I could do this?" When we follow the vision and the plan to get there, we can securely focus on that and not have to rely on our emotions.

When I jumped out of an airplane five times, I can tell you that I relied solely on the vision and plan, not my emotions. My emotions were all over the place. Fear, doubt, and anxiety washed over me and threatened to shut me down. Remembering the vision (goal) and the plan (training), I put the other stuff out of my mind and successfully executed my jump sequence and pulled my rip cord. This same dynamic has served me well when I started my business, wrote my first book, got my first TV special, and countless other moments. Go back to values, follow the vision—trust in those to stay motivated and not your emotions.

Allison Wise, LCSW, shocked everyone but herself when she left a high-paying job in the financial sector to pursue her true passion in serving others. She's been a social worker for over a decade and acknowledges the real threat of burnout to high-tempo servants. Allison says, "There's always too much to do, always a need, always something to fight for." She often returns to her values and vision when her motivation wanes.

Allison says that receiving mentorship and mentoring others helps keep her motivated and living the value of authenticity. Regarding her team, she feels it's important to "show them it's okay to be struggling and learning to say, 'I don't know.'" She says she "values clarity above all" and feels it draws people in and motivates them to get involved, not only with her team but with outside support as well. Having clear purpose and vision is exciting because it makes the goals much more real and doable.

Allison says that many people want to go into social services to help others, but when she owned her truth, saying, "I got into it to save myself and in the process, I serve others," her motivation ignited and that has sustained her. She also says it's vital to have a trust-based peer group that holds each other accountable to maintain motivation. Her team is constantly tested and purposefully check in with each other to see where their limits are, taking an assessment of supply and demand regarding motivation, because they simply can't do it all. She and her team have leveraged their motivation to motivate others and build a vision of a powerhouse social service unit, going from four people and a budget of $350,000 to twenty people and a budget of $3 million!

RAISE YOUR STANDARDS

One of the reasons our motivation can waver is because we're not challenging ourselves. Without the healthy tension of challenge, we can quickly fall into that rhythm-routine-rut dynamic I explained earlier. Raising our standards is something we alone can do, and we don't need anyone else's permission to do it.

There's a difference between good and great standards, but it all depends on what "great" really means to you. One of the funniest people I've ever known is Mike Pine, a classmate from the Air Force Academy. Mike is charismatic and gregarious, a natural people person. Mike was VP of marketing for the UFC for several years, working with Dana White and securing some of the first big sponsors UFC ever had, like Harley-Davidson and Burger King. But when we were cadets in the same class for glider training, it was apparent Mike would never be a pilot.

Mike was the last guy in our class of twenty to gain the confidence of his flight instructor that he was ready to solo the glider. It didn't take long to find out why. All of us students were able to watch his flight and could hear his radio calls, so he had a full audience. On his final approach he radioed the tower the famous line from *Top Gun.* "This is Ghost Rider, requesting a flyby." (Remember, these are gliders—you get only one shot to land.) He was admonished over the radio as we laughed.

The real excitement was yet to come. When Mike came down for final, he never flared, which is to pull the nose up to bleed off airspeed for landing. He went in like a lawn dart and bounced along with a huge cascade of dirt and debris from the unpaved airstrip. As his glider slid to a stop like a base runner sliding into second, we all took off running to see the chaos up close. The instructor led the way, screaming a tirade of expletives at full sprint. Mike emerged from the canopy and sat there with a wide smile, totally pleased with himself.

The instructor was turning purple with rage as his veins popped out of his head. "What the hell is the matter with you, Pine?"

Mike looked genuinely confused. "What? That was a great landing. I'm able to walk away."

The instructor screamed his retort. "*No*, dumbass, a great landing is where they can use the airplane again!"

What is your idea of great standards? Is it fulfilling your job description, pleasing your boss or the customers or clients you serve? Or is it something much more? We get to define our version of great and when we keep it challenging, we stay motivated by continually pushing ourselves to grow, develop, and deliver better and better results. Don't wait for someone else to do this for you. Do it for yourself.

CELEBRATE YOUR WINS

You're probably familiar with Pavlov's dog experiment: Ring the bell and the dog gets a treat, over and over again, until the dog is conditioned to expect a treat every time the bell rings. When she doesn't receive one, she's totally bummed out, whining and drooling . . . and waiting.

When we first start our careers, we're good at celebrating the moments like first day, first week, or first big project completed. Then over time, we go into head-down mode and just start grinding. We don't look up. We don't celebrate our achievements. And when that happens, we're actually conditioning ourselves not to care about achievements anymore. We finish something tough and instead of rewarding ourselves with a movie night, that new outfit, a spa day, or other treat, we shrug our shoulders and grunt an "oh well, on to the next thing." This squanders our motivation into the mud.

How fired up could we possibly be about the *next* thing if we're not even willing to celebrate the *now* thing? Take the time and make the choice to reward yourself for a job well done, condition yourself to care, and you'll develop your motivation when you do.

Invest in Your Mental Toughness

One of the best ways to keep our motivation strong when we're feeling weary, run-down, and depleted is the work we do on ourselves *before* we get to that point. Investing in our mental toughness by feeling our feelings, fostering joy, and practicing self-care inspires us to keep going when things become chaotic or overwhelming. Telling ourselves the right story about what we're going through, being tenacious, and recognizing our strength are also priceless in sustaining our motivation when it's tested.

Discipline is critical in life and business, but sometimes events cannot be outsmarted or outworked. What happens when we face a loss, a radical change, or the emotions from setbacks and disappointments? Perhaps the toughest challenge of this pandemic has been facing ambiguity and uncertainty. Though discipline helps keep our structure and schedule intact, it doesn't address the emotional pain so many are suffering. Discipline may harden us to endure, but mental toughness strengthens us to succeed.

The Japanese understood this concept in crafting the famous katana, the sword of samurai warriors and one of the finest-edged blades ever created by human hands. The katana incorporates both hardness (ability to stay rigid and *resist* impact) and toughness (ability to flex and *absorb* impact). Warriors need both as well because as Rocky, an icon of mental toughness, said so clearly, "It ain't about how hard you hit. It's about how hard you can get hit and keep moving forward."

ACKNOWLEDGE THE MOMENT AND "FEEL THE FEELINGS"

Mental toughness requires us to *develop emotional capacity* to deal with how we "feel." It requires humility, honesty, and vulnerability. And if we don't develop this, we're tempted to outrun or outwork our feelings. Like trying to get away from our own shadow, the solution is to stop running and shed light on it. We can ask "Where is this emotion coming from?" "Are these thoughts useful?" "What story am I telling myself right now?" or "Is that really true or just fear showing up?" This allows us to assess what's really going on. Our emotions left unchecked can wreak havoc. When things get internally chaotic, use this flipped-over call to action: Don't just do something . . . *sit there.* Examine it, process it, and move on.

FOSTER JOY

I see joy not as bubbly happiness, which is fleeting, but something much deeper and lasting. I like Merriam-Webster's definition: "the emotion evoked by well-being, success, or good fortune or by the prospect of possessing what one desires." It is a feeling of hope, optimism, gratitude for what we have and what's to come. Joy builds our capacity to deal with the inevitable setbacks and losses and the emotional pain that comes with them. Similar to the puffy "puffer jackets" that are in style again, joy insulates us from some of the pain during hard times, just as the jackets repel the cold. The more joy we foster, the puffier the jacket. Rod McKuen, one of my favorite poets, wrote "take the little times and make them into big times" when it comes to positive moments. That way, we have goodness in our memory banks to draw from during difficulties. Great life advice for fostering joy, especially in these times.

PRACTICE SELF-CARE

Self-care is more important than ever with the stressors we face. How can you serve anyone if you're falling apart physically or emotionally? Make the time, just like a business appointment, to do the things that are good for you: sleep, eat, exercise, meditate, read, watch funny movies, pray, do art, cook, or a million other things. The key is to know our own "stay well" ingredients and use them daily so we can recharge, just as a boxer does between rounds. This keeps us a warrior in the fight and prevents us from descending into a "worrier" like we discussed earlier. (We'll cover this much deeper in chapter 8.)

I've known Dr. Kevin Basik since I was seventeen years old. We're classmates from the U.S. Air Force Academy and he served his career as an award-winning instructor and educator, shaping the future of the Air Force officer corps, and understands the push and pull of those responsibilities. He's also one of the most motivated people I know, so it's no surprise he's visiting us in this chapter.

Kevin says, "I had a season where I was losing myself in

the flurry of activity. I was doing my best to deliver but feeling more and more drained. Depleted. My fitness was put on the back burner, conversations with my family were surface level and sporadic, and I'd stopped investing in friendships. As a result, I was losing the passion, connection, and commitment that fueled my work. I was feeling more and more like I wasn't all there." Kevin was approaching burnout and he felt it.

Regarding how the warrior spirit relates at times like these, he says, "For me, the warrior spirit is about clarity of identity. It's who we strive to be while the storms are howling. When times get hard, it's the proving ground for our character. I've had moments of heartbreak, betrayal, embarrassment, abject fear, and failure. I seldom had control over why those happened, but I sure had a choice about how I would respond. The warrior spirit is tethered to the values we're willing to fight to bring to life. To borrow from my friend and leadership coach Kari Granger, the question is not 'Are you a warrior?' but 'What are you a warrior for?'"

Kevin made a hard pivot to get back into alignment by realizing the truth—we can't be a warrior when we're falling apart. He decided that if he didn't deposit "an investment into myself—to include my health, family, and friendships—then I was racing towards bankruptcy of the soul." His workouts became sacred. Family dinners were prioritized. He invested in conversations with his wife, kids, and friends. He says, "And wouldn't you know it, I showed up more complete and valuable for those I was serving."

TELL YOURSELF A BETTER STORY

The narratives we tell ourselves are critical to our success, level of happiness, fulfillment, performance, and every other aspect of who we are and what we do. Stories are not only created, but they can be changed. What happens to us is neutral to the bigger universe, but the story we tell ourselves about what it means to us creates our own narrative and holds power in our lives. You can get a good and quick sense of how this works when you talk to people about their challenges. Some will say the setbacks, disappointments, or stumbles toward their goal led them to become better and understand more why they wanted it. Others will describe those same dynamics as a "sign it wasn't meant to be" or some other justification to change direction or quit.

We've all heard of PTSD—post-traumatic stress disorder—but there is also post-traumatic growth. According to Dr. Martin Seligman, some of the key points to creating this dynamic is the narrative we tell ourselves when hard things happen. In our own lives, we live up—or down—to the stories we tell ourselves. Crazy Horse, the famous Lakota warrior, believed that he would never be killed by white men's bullets. He lived his life believing that and it led to some of the legendary moments of courage he displayed. What story do you tell yourself about your ability, power, potential, and past events? Tell yourself a better story—and then live it.

Kevin shared a great discovery in dealing with adversity and setbacks, which can be threats to our motivation and mental toughness. He says, "One of the resources we often overlook in times of suffering are the people around us. The biggest lie we tell ourselves (aka the story) when we're in the battles of life is 'I am alone in this struggle.'" He learned this when he and his wife were having heartbreaking fertility issues for five years. They kept it to themselves, and he says, "It followed us everywhere like a dark cloud on a tether. We convinced ourselves that no one else had these issues, couldn't understand, and shouldn't be burdened with our pain." But after a mentor encouraged him to share a bit of their story, the floodgates of support opened up. Kevin now leans on this dynamic to stay motivated and mentally tough when facing work challenges, feelings of overwhelm, or personal or professional setbacks. It works like a charm for him and can for you as well.

Kevin also shared a hilarious use of the stories we tell ourselves when dealing with a negative label or judgment by others. "I entered the six weeks of Basic Cadet Training (BCT) at the Air Force Academy with a target painted on my chest. Actually, it was right above the right pocket where your name goes. Rule #1 during BCT is 'Don't do anything to draw attention to yourself.' My name is Basik—pronounced 'basic.' It just so happens that during BCT all trainees are addressed as 'Basic (your name here).' You can do the math. I'm 'Basic Basik.' The story I was telling myself was that I was going to get continual flak and be miserable. So I changed the story. I came up with a battle cry that the upperclassmen cadre would have me shout when they wanted a chuckle." Kevin embraced what could've been a negative and would scream with pride,

"Six weeks? Hell, I've been a Basic my whole life!" How could you flip the script when you get judged, categorized, or diminished? We all have opportunities to make these moments of temporary weakness into an enduring strength. Kevin became one of the most popular and celebrated trainees in BCT—and ultimately in our class too.

The last thing Kevin shared about motivation was a gem that was borrowed from expectancy theory by Victor Vroom. Paraphrased, it says that people are motivated by an equation that multiplies three perceptions that create a story: (1) Can I do it? Do I perceive I can pull off the level of performance I need to succeed? (2) If I do succeed in this action, will the outcome promised actually be there? (3) Do I value the outcome? Kevin says, "The higher each of these is, the more compelling the story, and the more likely I'll be motivated to dedicate effort and energy. But, because this is multiplied, if any of these go to zero, the whole thing goes to zero and my motivation will bottom out." So it's important that we are aware of these questions, their answers, and the story they tell us if we're trying to create sustained motivation in the work we do.

BE TENACIOUS

In our Native cultures, we admire our four-legged and winged relatives and try to emulate their best qualities. They are our teachers that instruct us how to live our best lives when we represent the strength of a bear, the vision of an eagle, or the family loyalty shown by wolves. Our people and warriors depended on these animal guides when they faced struggles. When times get tough and our motivation wanes, we need to dig in and be tenacious. When it comes to tenacity, I can't think of a better example than the wolverine (not the one with goofy hair played by Hugh Jackman). Wolverines are not known for their size, speed, or good looks. In fact, they're small, grumpy, and stinky. They're known for being the baddest mofo in whatever valley they're in. They're only the size of a medium dog, but have thick hide, sharp claws, powerful jaws, and a unique tenacity in the animal world. They can go anywhere, up cliffs and over ice, and travel up to fifteen miles a day to find food. They eat anything, from stealing bird eggs to hunting deer, which outsize them by many times. And they seem to fear nothing and are known to frequently scare bears and wolf packs away.

When times get hard, we must adopt the spirit of a wolverine. Dig in. Take the next step, the next breath. Don't turn away or quit. Hang in there to finish the project, confront a tough situation, or just get through that hard day. Our motivation gets a huge boost when we take this approach and see it through. Tomorrow will be a new day and we'll get there if we're tenacious.

RECOGNIZE YOUR STRENGTH

Everyone is being tested, enduring their own ceremony of transformation. You may at times be fatigued, weary, heartbroken, and even tempted to curl up or throw in the towel. But you've been through tough times before and made it. You're stronger than you know. Mental toughness keeps us in the fight and committed to our purpose—especially when it's hard or feels impossible—and doesn't require working faster or doing more. Sometimes it means letting go for a moment to dig deep and summon your warrior spirit, opening the floodgate of intense positive energy that fills you up as you draw strength from your ancestors, the universe itself, and growl, "I am a warrior and I will not quit. I will find a way forward!" And even if there are tears in your eyes as you say it . . . you are.

⸪

We're our own firekeepers and responsible for keeping our fires (aka motivation) burning through all circumstances. Motivation is not automatic and it's up to us to consistently create the right kind for ourselves, on purpose and with purpose. Seeing all the ways we can do that keeps us at the ready to have another log to throw on the fire when it's diminished. Investing in our mental toughness, and making it a priority, allows us to stay strong through challenges, overwhelm, and chaos so we can fulfill our warrior roles.

7

Read the Signs and Stay Vigilant

A Warrior's Work Is Never Done

t was apparent Lisa had a chip on her shoulder. She acted as if she no longer needed advice or coaching, those elements that enable us to keep learning and growing. Lisa came from an organization of practitioners where speed was valued over accuracy, and Dr. Jonathan Baines (Tsimshian/Tlingit), a teaching doctor and family practitioner at the Mayo Clinic, worried about that mindset in a medical setting. He told me, "A critical understanding to be good at what we do is knowing what we know—but also knowing what we *don't* know." He readily admits no one is immune to error, but Lisa had that dangerous trait that could spell disaster for her patients: arrogance.

One day, a man in his forties came in to see Lisa. He was

in obvious pain, sweating and grunting through his breaths, all from severe lower back pain. After a rushed assessment without any other consultation, she gave him a round of antibiotics for a kidney infection. The man returned a week later, still in crisis, barely able to walk, and doubled over in pain. Lisa dismissively prescribed another round of antibiotics for him. Another week passed and the patient was thoroughly reassessed by another practitioner. They found a painful pinched nerve in the lower thoracic area—not a kidney infection. The man suffered for almost two weeks without relief until the proper diagnosis was rendered.

Knowledge is not power. We all know people who know how to improve and yet they don't, people who knew the right thing to do but did the wrong thing anyway. Sometimes, that was us. So we know that knowledge is *not* power. *Applied* knowledge is power. It's not what we learn or know that impacts our lives, careers, or service to others. It's how we *use* those ideas that makes a difference.

Dr. Baines has seen moments like this in his career where a combination of arrogance, ignorance, and an unwillingness to stay humble and keep growing can cause frustration, pain, or worse, for patients seeking help. In the same way, imagine how valuable of an asset we can become when we continue to grow and learn. To be a warrior who effectively delivers in your role, you must keep up your skill set, knowledge, and abilities through continuous practice and lifetime learning.

This is how our warriors of the past always operated too. Our warriors submitted themselves to a lifetime process of development, growth, and learning from others and their own experiences that started in childhood. A warrior constantly trained to improve their abilities and adapt new tactics through relentless practice, hunting, and raiding. They toughened their bodies through running, riding, games, and frequent deprivation. They created a resilient spirit through ceremony, guidance and coaching from elders, and prayer. They learned how to forage off the land, build and repair weapons and tools, communicate and coordinate with other warriors, and start a fire in any condition. They gained not only muscle memory but wisdom in all these processes and eventually became elders, the ones who shared their treasure trove of learning with the tribe (but more on that in chapter 10).

Warriors kept the unwavering, obsessive goal in mind of constantly improving themselves to better deliver in their role, an Indigenous model of continuous improvement. Part of this training was learning to practice silence, awareness, and observation. Our warriors had an almost mystical ability to read signs. In fact, when the Europeans first arrived, they thought our people were magical because of this ability. Through careful and consistent observation, our warriors could read signs through disturbed wildlife, vegetation, or ground and through smells or sounds to detect and track enemies. They could predict weather and migration patterns, knew when things would bud, bloom, or fruit. It was about being aware but also being connected to and deeply engaged with the environment itself. Our warriors paid attention to

everything they could see, feel, hear, or smell. They were totally engaged and immersed in their environments, which allowed them to make strategic decisions, avoid threats, or
attack decisively.

We live in a constant state of stimulus, distraction, and
information overload—this is the norm, not the exception.
It's easy to get paralyzed by the bombardment of messages
and become checked out or navigate on autopilot. It's a challenge to not become the disengaged person we've all seen,
who walks and talks with earbuds so immersed in their heads
that they don't pay attention to people around them. Or the
car that runs them over.

Think of how many things are automated or marvels of
technology that allow us to not think so much. We have cars
that park themselves, books are read to us, we push buttons
for food, and even the bathrooms operate themselves. I was in
a busy bathroom at a conference where the toilets, sinks, and
paper towel dispensers were automated. My confusion led to
the other patrons' frustration when I kept waving my hands
under the soap dispenser in every conceivable way. A guy
reached in front of me to put his hand on it and said, "Look,
man, you just pump it."

The other downside to lack of awareness is that it allows our
skill sets to become stale or irrelevant. It leads to the pattern
we covered earlier of getting into a rhythm, then a routine . . .
then a rut. Realizing that we live in a dynamic age, the information age where change is a constant, we're reminded that if
we're serious about becoming the best version of ourselves,

then school is never out for us and we must commit to being lifetime learners. The war cry here is "Improve!" Just as a blade needs to be resharpened or a bow restrung, our skill sets need to be constantly honed, updated, and resharpened so we stay effective. We don't want to ride our one-trick pony until his hooves fall off. When we stay in a constant state of learning and growth, we stay evergreen in our development. And effectiveness. A great lesson from nature reminds us that we can fall prey to overspecialization or rigid thinking or become myopic in our views when we ignore change and stop improving. And we do so at our own peril.

Lesson of the Lynx

The thirty-pound cat moves like a ghost through the snow-covered forest in Montana. Stalking silently on oversize feet, designed to be natural snowshoes, the lynx is on the lookout for its singular prey—the snowshoe hare. The lynx is endowed with a superathletic ability that seems to defy physics. It is cunning, quiet, fast, and deadly. So why is this cat in such deep trouble?

The lynx in Montana was thought to number some three thousand in the late 1990s, but the results of a more recent study, which I read about in *Smithsonian* magazine, found a dismal figure of only around three hundred. Despite its natural gifts, the lynx has been a victim of tough times—deforestation, a warmer climate that has negated its incredible advantage to hunt in snow—but most importantly, an increased competition with other predators over its one and only food source, the snowshoe hare. Regardless of the lynx's talents, its overspecialization is leading to its demise in Montana. Meanwhile, the lynx's cousins, the mountain lion and bobcat, are opportunists who eat whatever prey is available. They are both faring well despite the dynamic changes.

It is easy to get complacent and overly focused on the things we're good at doing, but we can get caught when the world around us changes the conditions. Especially in tough times, we must stay flexible, be willing to change, gather new resources, adapt and grow. But take heart, even in the hardest of times, opportunities can be found (or created) with this approach. IBM became a powerhouse company during the Great Depression. A close friend of mine saw her layoff as a golden opportunity to go back to school for her PhD. What challenge are you going through that you could twist and shape into success?

Take time to read to stay current, find ways to diversify your opportunities, take your projects in different directions, and look for gold veins in the dark caves. Invest in your relationships, go to coffee with a colleague, tap your social networks to find opportunities. Grab some downtime to take a walk or go on a hike or a retreat to get your mojo and perspective back. It is often during these quiet moments where we have life- and career-changing breakthroughs. Whatever we've got to do to keep from viewing the world and our problems through a soda straw, we must do. Otherwise, we may find ourselves, like the lynx, cruising quietly over the snow and hunting intently . . . for what's no longer there.

Requirements for a Lifetime of Learning

Just as we prepare for a job, an athletic competition, or travels to make the outcome more successful, we prepare ourselves to become lifetime learners by highlighting some effective strategies that get results. These ideas are simple and practical and will keep you in learning mode, continually adding to your fund of knowledge.

STAY HUMBLE

Humility is not only one of our most important and enduring values in tribal communities, it is the key to lifetime growth. Without it, we shut the doors to the schoolhouse and stop learning. We've all met these people (sometimes we *are* these people) who have that "been there, done that, nothing new under the sun" attitude. Arrogance and ego lead us to stagnation. Humility reminds us that it's okay to not have all the answers. It allows us to keep asking questions, just like we did when we were kids, so we can keep learning throughout our lives and careers. There is always room to grow and improve.

Remember, we continue this process not to only benefit and better ourselves, but to better and benefit those we serve.

When we stay humble, there's no limit to how much we can learn, or how good we can become at who we are and what we do.

Holly Figueroa (Hopi) is a warrior in the health and wellness arena. She works for a large healthcare system in Arizona and has been a passionate and committed advocate for delivering vital services to both tribal communities and Native veterans for many years. Holly is humble and constantly working on herself to be able to contribute more deeply to those she serves. Yet she harbors an insecurity. She told me, "I am super grateful for having a career as a tribal liaison. I would have never thought that I would be in a position where I can work to help serve tribal members of all walks of life. I say this because I don't have postsecondary education. Knowing I don't have all the credentials that my colleagues have, I work very hard to be informed and have the tools to continue to be successful."

Holly doesn't let her lack of higher degrees stop her from pursuing an education. She regularly attends professional development groups, stays engaged in her support network, and is always working on her own skill sets and knowledge base and intentionally gaining new experiences. Holly is a wonderful example of turning a vulnerability into a strength and an insecurity into an asset.

Ask yourself, what areas of your life or development have you tended to avoid because you feel vulnerable or sensitive to them? How could you acknowledge, humbly accept, and leverage them so you can move forward on your developmental journey? Maybe the time you were fired shouldn't be seen as just a disappointment, but as a priceless moment of learning and transformation. Maybe the criticism you receive from a toxic boss or client can be fuel to recommit to your growth. Maybe your current lack of titles, designations, or education can be seen not as a lack at all, but as an asset, allowing you to see, explore, and innovate without the expectations attached to those things.

BECOME AN ASTUTE OBSERVER

Just as our warriors depended on vigilant awareness, reading signs and patterns to make good decisions, we need to follow the same dynamic to stay relevant and capable in our own world. This is much less complicated than it sounds. All you have to do is reduce stimuli—slow down and stop multitasking. We are often moving so fast, doing so much, because we're so worried about missing something that we're actually missing everything. Sit, watch, listen. Do this frequently and intentionally during your day. You'll be amazed at what you learn. You'll be better able to spot trends, grab opportunities or create them, avoid pitfalls, collaborate with strategic partners, and continue your forward momentum.

When we can see what's coming, then we choose whether to be reactive or proactive. Being reactive is waiting for the forcing function to move us to act. Every year in Colorado it snows. Everyone knows it's coming. And yet everyone waits until the first snow and then it takes a week to get the snow tires put on at the shop because of the crowd. How do I know this? Well, I'm not saying.

Being proactive is seeing the trend or expecting the change and then acting on it. For instance, when we're planning a vacation, we know the longer we take to get tickets, the more expensive they become and the less availability for seating. We have a real incentive to act before the changes occur.

HAVE BETTER CONVERSATIONS

There are few conversation topics that drain the life force right out of me like the weather. It's boring and awkward and takes way too long, providing little to no interesting information. The quality of our conversations leads to a quality impact on its participants. For instance, having an interesting topic or question as a focal point often defines the direction of the discussion and people are more likely to exchange valuable, useful knowledge or information. Learning happens. Asking interesting questions like "What do you think inspires people to higher levels of creativity?" instead of discussing the weather, is going to determine a very different conversation. When people can walk away with new ideas or be reminded of good ones, there's a much higher benefit than discussing what the low temperature was last night.

This is also why it's so important to have activities, to read, to stay current, engaged, and learning. Interesting people are interested in the world around them. This practice ensures that we can offer ideas to others and create interactions that trigger insights, breakthroughs, and growth.

BE MORE INTROSPECTIVE

Ever have a stack of papers you need to shred and impatiently feed too many in at once? It's a recipe for a frustrating paper jam. In the same way, trying to process all the ideas we take in each day has a similar dynamic, causing overwhelm or mental paralysis. Instead, we need to set aside time, or several points during the day, where we can process and contemplate what we've learned. Carve out some quiet time to review what you're learning and why it matters. You can discuss the ideas with colleagues, take a short walk and mentally review them, or journal the ideas for permanent capture. I carry a trusty "brain book" wherever I go and jot down useful thoughts, ideas, tips, quotes, or recommended books. These brain books have been transformative in my life and business. The number of ideas we are exposed to doesn't have nearly as much impact as the ideas we *process* to learn and understand. The quality and effectiveness of our days rises quickly when we do this.

RAISE THE ROOF

We are all responsible for our own level of effort—not our boss, employer, or client. And that choice can lead us to excellence or mediocrity. In the story of the Three Little Pigs, the pigs are trying to build a structure to protect against the wolf. No offense, but we are the pigs. The wolf is hard times, lay-offs, disappointments, and setbacks.

The first pig builds his house of straw. These are the people who do the bare minimum, just enough to keep their jobs. Their house looks solid, but it's image over substance. The wolf shows up and blows it down.

The second pig builds his house of sticks. This is the person who does enough to stay off the boss's radar. They do their job, a "good enough" job, but not one smidge beyond job description. The wolf shows up and blows the house down.

The third pig builds her house of bricks. She does what she says she'll do, is a team player, and goes above and beyond not because she's told to, but because she *wants* to. She gets a kick out of delivering her best and growing her capacity. And she does it with a smile. She's made herself into a valuable asset, a must-have teammate, and has a reputation for excellence. When the wolf comes to her house, he's out of luck. Raising our standards and committing to our best effort each day is our best protection from the wolf.

My friend Jacob had a career as an educator, as both a veteran teacher and school principal, before he decided to become an employee of his tribe. Then he wanted to continue elevating his contributions, so he applied to a leadership position. But his intentions came to a screeching halt when someone else got the position. His new boss, feeling threatened, started to blatantly micromanage Jacob and then sidelined him, cutting him out of the loop and disinviting him from a personal development course. Jacob was frustrated, upset, and confounded.

Instead of lamenting, Jacob doubled down on his own development and started watching video recordings of the course. He listened to personal development podcasts on the weekends, consistently consulting with a tribal elder for advice and encouragement. He stayed focused on improving himself so he could "contribute to the max."

Jacob looks at this process as another extension of the traditional warrior role. He told me, "You're there to provide resources and serve your people—we're not hunting and fishing every day, but we're still going to a job to provide resources for our families and those we serve." Jacob turned his disappointment into triumph by following this mindset, consciously setting an example for his people of how to respond during adversity. The result? He was eventually appointed as senior manager of operational excellence for his entire organization. He now has a bigger platform, more impact, and deeper fulfillment in the contribution he continues to make to his people.

BE PATIENT

Patience is a vital necessity in lifelong learning, yet it's challenging to practice it in a world where the speed of life is the speed of light. Movies like *The Matrix* don't help things, when the main character, Neo, can simply plug his head into a machine and within a few seconds he knows kung fu. Of course, we know learning doesn't work that way, but how many times have we caught ourselves thinking it does (or should)? We must keep the long game in mind and know that if we keep growing and developing ourselves through lifetime learning, our contribution to our tribe grows and develops too.

My friend Juanita Mullen is a great example of this dynamic in action. Juanita is a member of the Seneca Tribe, proud Air Force veteran, cancer survivor, and a woman full of initiative, fight, and the warrior spirit. She's a tribal liaison for the Department of Veterans Affairs and coordinates services for Native American veterans, ensuring that they get the care to which they're entitled. She works with over 574 federally recognized tribes and over 200 state-recognized tribes, which requires intensive research to learn the nuances and differences in all the tribal communities she serves. It takes a lot of time and a lot of patience.

This type of ongoing learning doesn't just make her more capable at her job, it also shows respect for the mission and those she serves. Juanita told me, "I'm always learning. Just because one has a bachelor's or master's degree, the learning doesn't stop there. These degrees have to be maintained. Despite all the books I've read on history, science, archaeology, and literature, I'm still learning. As you go along, it makes life just a little bit easier with the knowledge you gain."

When we better understand the world around us, we better know where we fit into it. And when we better understand the people we serve, we can serve them better.

FIND A ROLE MODEL

It's tragic that so many people I've talked to over the years believe that role models are relevant only in our childhoods. We need role models in every stage of our lives because we all need someone to look up to. We need to identify which qualities we'd like to emulate and which behaviors we'd like to mirror on our own journey. Emulating a role model is not a push to be someone else, it's a pull to gravitate toward targets we choose when it comes to values, behaviors, and examples.

Ask yourself, who are your role models and why? What are the good qualities that draw you to them? What good examples do they display that make them worthy role models for you? When we have answers to these questions, we have more reminders and road signs on our journey to keep us growing and developing into what and who we want to become.

TRIBE UP—WARRIORS NEVER FIGHT ALONE

Our warriors always fought in the company of other warriors. Their true strength came not from their independence but from their interdependence, which provided them with strength, support, relief, and the encouragement to fostered bravery and lifetime learning. Plus, enduring the challenges as a group strengthened their bonds of trust and teamwork, which strengthened the overall tribe.

We all need this on our journey as well. A common philosophy in our Native cultures is that we are all connected—that doesn't mean just your family, teammates, or colleagues. It means all people, plants, animals, the whole earth, and the universe itself. If you're walking your journey alone, you're doing it wrong! Leverage your connections to both draw and offer strength. I was taught we're more like ants and bees than eagles, social creatures by design, neurologically hardwired for connection. We need each other, and we're better when we're with the right people.

The Haudenosaunee, also known as People of the Long-house and the Six Nations Iroquois Confederacy, is a group of tribal nations (Seneca, Cayuga, Mohawk, Onondaga, Tuscarora, and Oneida) that banded together in unity for mutual strength, protection, and growth. The legend goes that Hiawatha, who spoke on behalf of the Peacemaker, a prophet and holy man, united the tribes by showing them how easy it was to break one arrow. He then tied a bundle of arrows together and asked the chiefs present to break it. None of them could. We can create this same dynamic when we surround ourselves with the tribe we create. We become stronger, smarter, more resilient, more capable, and better. We become unbreakable.

The quickest way I've seen to become a happy, healthy person and a high performer is to hang out with those types of people. The quickest way I've seen to become a complainer, gossiper, or fear-based or negative person is to hang out with those folks. It's painfully simple but frequently ignored. The thing we must remember is we choose our flock and must choose wisely. Zig Ziglar had a wonderful quote: "It's hard to fly like an eagle if you're surrounded by turkeys."

If I asked you to close your eyes, turn in a circle a few times, and then point to the north, would you guess correctly? We require outside visual cues because we don't work like other creatures in nature—say, for instance, pigeons. Pigeons were given a gift by the Creator at birth, a set of molecules that line up in their brains to show them where true north is. It's an internal, fail-safe GPS system. They never get lost! We don't work that way. Ever made a dumb decision . . . or I'm alone in that? We're human beings, we make bad calls, we make mistakes, we can lose sight of where we're headed, so we need to surround ourselves with the right flock, our own tribe, to remind us of our direction—and help us get there. My friend and fellow speaker Dr. Kevin Basik says, "Show me your friends and I'll show you your future." We get to choose our tribe and we want to make sure we're choosing one that is heading in the direction we prefer and developing in ways we'd like to develop ourselves.

When you start and continue to develop yourself, to grow into who you were meant to be, you'll attract others who are like-minded. A dynamic I've experienced, and you probably have too, is that *like attracts like*. If you've ever done the experiment of making rock candy as a kid, you'll remember having a glass full of boiling water and sugar with a pencil across the top of the glass with a string hanging down. As the sugar cools, it collects on the string in crystalline structures that form rock candy. We didn't push the string around to chase the sugar (and it doesn't work any better if we do). The string attracts the sugar instead. When we chase connections, they can be elusive and the process of chasing them can become exhausting. But when we work on developing ourselves, our character, vision, skills, and direction, we draw others in. We attract like-minded folks like sugar to the string.

PLAY

Warriors didn't just show up one day on the field of battle and expect victory. They trained and developed into that role and a big part of it was *play*. Warriors in tribal communities were groomed to develop their skills from childhood with toys like junior version bows and arrows and wooden knives, and games like shooting arrows through rolling hoops, mock battles, wrestling, and running contests. In fact, the popular Native American stickball game played in many versions by many tribes, now known as lacrosse, is called "the little brother of war." It prepared warriors for battle on a nonlethal field of play and was a mix of football, hockey, rugby, and UFC—exhausting, brutal, thrilling, and requiring strategy, physical skill, teamwork, and bravery.

When we play, we get to learn and master critical skill sets in a low-threat, low-stakes environment. Those risks that so often shut down learning new things or sticking with them can include intimidation, fear of judgment, criticism, and the shame of making mistakes. I remember a comment from Doug, my Krav Maga instructor, when I was frustrated and struggling to execute a new move. He came up to me smiling and said, "Don't worry about it. I want to allow you not only to feel success but failure too. Otherwise, you can't know if your move truly works." I immediately relaxed and was able to learn it.

Play releases us from our shackles and we become more and more skilled as we play our way into some serious growth in skill and capacity. And we enjoy the process of learning much more as well.

How do you play?

In order to add play into your role, organize your responsibilities so you can "level up," and reward yourself whenever you do. For me, I enjoy playing RTS (real-time strategy) games like *Medieval II* and *Dawn of Man*, where you build up resources and capacity. There's a special joy in leveling up. In the games, you grow and store food, build things, improve technologies or social structures to take better care of your people. I love that. I've always seen my skills development and building my business in much the same way.

Anyone who knows me, knows I'm playful onstage, but I've also made securing contracts and sales, one of the toughest parts of business, into something playful as well. I keep track of it on a spreadsheet created by my friend, mentor, and fellow speaker and writer Mark LeBlanc. I play it like a game, racking up points with each booking, contract, or project. It keeps an otherwise intimidating grind in the fun zone for me. What works for you to keep your work fun?

One of the keys to building a stronger warrior spirit is to

make what we do fun. Why? This allows us to stay light on our toes, resilient, creative, and quicker to find solutions and to rebound when we feel we've been knocked sideways. It also makes it a lot more fun to be around, which makes it easier to collaborate and partner with other people and share ideas as well. Collaborate to share the war stories of noteworthy victories, even the tiniest ones, but also the hilarious moments of making mistakes, learning, and recovering with your friends and inner circle.

The Power of Accountability

To be a lifelong learner who prioritizes self-development, we need to surround ourselves with a tribe that keeps us on point and holds us accountable to our commitments when things get hard or chaotic or we feel run-down or defeated. When left to our own devices, many of us are tempted to do the bare minimum—or least not nearly as much as what we're capable of doing. This is why CEOs, athletes, and actors hire coaches, why those who want to get fit hire trainers, and why those who want to deliver their best surround themselves with a tribe they create on purpose.

Our tribe can include family, elders, friends, colleagues, and personal or professional development groups. When we surround ourselves with people who offer us great examples, encouragement, advice, and the expectation that we are capable of greater things, we quickly rise accordingly. When we have a tribe who can help us recognize our own bullshit, or call us out when we're out of alignment with our values or goals, we can correct course. Without accountability, it is easier to walk away or change directions when (not if, but when) things get tough or uncomfortable. Having people who hold each other mutually accountable keeps the whole tribe on course.

I remember the challenge of writing my first book, *The Tiny Warrior*. I was struggling and dragging my feet, doubtful about the whole project, when I connected with Dr. April Lea Go Forth (Cherokee), a meeting planner who was hosting a conference early the next year. We became friends over the course of several months of working together. Once we were about six months away from the conference, she asked me about the book I mentioned I was working on and said matter-of-factly, "We'll look forward to having your book at our conference." My heart skipped a beat as she continued, "It'll be ready by then, right?"

Suddenly my mouth was dry and without thinking it through, I blurted a response: "Yes, it will."

And that woman called me every month to check on my progress until I got it completed! She encouraged me, cajoled me, and laid out her preconceived wonderful attributes of the book I was writing. I have an acknowledgment in the book to April Lea Go Forth for "lighting a fire of great expectations and then holding my feet to it." That is the power of accountability.

When we stop seeking or accepting support, we put ourselves into a corner that can quickly become dark, lonely, and stressful. We all need support because we all struggle at times.

_·'·_

Warriors used the power of observation and awareness to become almost mystical in their ability to read signs and understand what happened, what is now, and what will be. This meant they spent a lifetime in development, original models of continuous improvement. If we are to be fully engaged in our role, we too must stay sharp; we too must keep growing and developing for a lifetime.

8

Use Your Medicine to Heal

*Creating the Right Environment
for Sustained Strength*

Karen was in the middle of a training for tribal employees when suddenly she couldn't form words. She was struggling to even form thoughts. She had been dealing with a lot of stress from work, family, and serving on boards and had just experienced the sudden loss of a beloved sister. The unaddressed stress had reached critical mass.

Despite experiencing the warning signs of a health problem, Karen ignored them all. Later, she told me, "I passed them off as 'no big deal, I'll be all right.' I just kept pushing myself. Even on the day of the stroke, I didn't want to quit—so I stayed the night and got up to finish the training the next day. I could not and did not deliver great service, and it made me feel terrible."

A few days later, Karen experienced another ministroke. This time, she called her doctor and was instructed to go straight to the ER, where she was promptly admitted. It was a terrifying near miss that rocked her to her core, and afterward her mindset changed. Karen realized how important it was to take care of herself first. Her healing took several months and multiple doctor appointments, medications, rest . . . and new-found patience, now that she had experienced the impacts of self-neglect firsthand. She says, "I already knew how fragile life could be, so if things were going to change, I had to change in order to get back to my work and doing what I love most."

Warriors Aren't Bulletproof

Like so many who have dedicated their lives to serving others, we can run into disaster when we stop protecting and caring for ourselves first. Our intentions to serve may be noble and pure—but intentions be damned. It's execution that matters!

Yes, a warrior is someone who develops their talent and ability over a lifetime to become a true asset to the tribe they serve. Our tribal warriors fought against incredible odds and showed heroic levels of strength, courage, and resiliency. However, *our warriors weren't bulletproof*! And neither are you.

Though we often romanticize the role of our Native American warriors into an unachievable, unattainable image of a perfect, stoic person without needs, we too often forget that our warriors faced periods of fear, stress, and doubt. This same oversight affects those in the helping professions. Our warriors of the past also struggled, made mistakes, felt frustration, and sometimes stumbled, fell, or cried—but they did not quit. Knowing they weren't bulletproof kept them grounded and made it easier to seek the support, encouragement, self-care, and resources they needed to fulfill their roles.

In the same way, when we refuse to be open to outside resources or support, we set ourselves up for burnout. That's what a martyr does. Martyrs go, go, go until they fall apart and can't serve anyone anymore, standing back confused and asking, "What the hell happened to me?" A warrior does what's necessary, including getting help, rest, and self-care, so they can stay strong in their role and serve others well. We need warriors in the world, not martyrs.

In my tribe, the Ottawa Tribe of Michigan, there are two ways of learning: kendoswin, or head learning, and bokadwin, or heart learning. Kendoswin is useful and needed in the world. It's logic, using facts to solve problems—think of Mr. Spock in *Star Trek*. Bokadwin, on the other hand, is using quiet to tap our intuition and hear our internal voice—think Captain Kirk, who so often acted on his gut instincts. Bokadwin allows us access to our intuition, a gut feeling, that little whisper that comes to us when we're quiet and tells us things like "Slow down," "Take a break," "Get some rest," "Eat something," or "Get some help or advice." We ignore this guiding voice at our own peril, especially when it's trying to guide us to deal with our stresses in a healthy, productive way. When we do this, we suffer needlessly and hurt our ability to serve others. We can't be warriors when we're falling apart.

To be a warrior who effectively delivers in your role, you must manage your stress not by striving to eliminate it, but by striving to create balance. Balance is a universal philosophy in our tribal belief system. It says that there is a day for night, there is joy and pain, the seasons change to balance the land, there are victories and setbacks, and there should be activity and rest. Even the simple act of breathing reminds us over and over again of the cycle of rejuvenation after depletion. We breathe in, breathe out, and restore balance. However, try to breathe in for as long as you can. Breathe in, breathe in, breathe . . . silly, right? But if we breathe in, breathe out, breathe in, breathe out, we restore balance and strength and now we're ready for the fight ahead. Meanwhile, the person who kept breathing in is passed out and useless to everyone now.

Most of us know *how* to take good care of ourselves and manage our stress—we just don't actually *do* it. We've all heard the announcement on flights to put your oxygen mask on first if the cabin depressurizes. But how many of you reading this have ever felt a twinge of guilt about doing that? After all, if the person you love most in the world, your spouse, your child, is sitting in the seat next to you, isn't putting your own mask on first . . . selfish? As much as we complain about airlines, they've got this one right. Regardless of your intentions or how much you love someone else, you can't help or serve anyone if you're incapacitated. Put your own mask on first. Take care of yourself first. And *then* you'll be able to serve others well. Eliminate the fear that taking care of yourself will make you selfish. It won't. But it sure will make you happier and more resilient. And taking care of yourself first (and best) is the highest form of care you can provide for others because if you can do it for you first, you can then do it for others.

Working with so many big-hearted service providers for many years, I've heard the craziest things I've ever heard come out of the mouths of those in healthcare, education, or community services. We'll do full-day sessions on self-care and without exception, someone will come up afterward and say, "D.J., this is great stuff and I really appreciate it. I'm going to start doing these things too!" And then a pause before I hear these gems: *Next year, when my kids are grown, when this project is done, when it's not so busy.* And this zinger I still chuckle about: "Don't worry about me, I've got a vacation scheduled in seven years." And we wonder why stress can derail us.

Is Stress Always Bad?

I often have conversations where people lament the stresses they're under and wish that they had none. But that's not the goal! What do we call people with zero stress? Yep, dead. That is literally the only way we're getting out of experiencing stress. If we're a living creature on this planet, whether a salmon, an eagle, an oak tree, or a human being, we're going to have some stress. Some stress is natural, necessary, and needed. And in the right amount, stress is beneficial.

I once read an article about the reintroduction of the gray wolf into Yellowstone National Park. The project leader, Ed Bangs with the U.S. Fish and Wildlife Service, said that when they introduced wolves back into their natural habitats, they didn't just get better wolves. They got better elk too. When elk don't have a natural stressor in their environment, like wolves as a predator, they don't act like wild animals anymore (i.e., vigilant, aware, survival focused). Instead, they act more like livestock—ho-hum and on autopilot.

The point is, if we look at stress as the wolf, we don't need to curse the wolf or try to eliminate the wolf—we need the wolf! We just don't need a whole pack of them on our heels. That's the trick, trying to manage our stress. And when we do, it can actually work for us.

Have you ever felt in "the zone" or in a state of "flow"? This is when stress is actually serving us. Do you work well against a deadline? Of course, most of us do, that's why more work gets done in the three days before a vacation than the previous three weeks. The stress provides clarity so we know what to say yes to and what to say no to (or "not now" to). With the right amount of stress, we can be more productive, effective, and in our zone—and it feels great.

Imagine a bell curve starting flat on a baseline at 0 percent (i.e., dead), rising to a peak and then dropping off and flattening out again back to the baseline at 100 percent (i.e., on the way to dead). This is how stress works in our lives. The right kind of stress brings us to the peak. But once we start to add more to our plates, that's where the problems begin as we slide over the top of the curve onto the other side known as *distress*. This is where stress starts to have wonky effects on us, causing problems with our work, our relationships, and even our health.

Another way to see stress is like a fireplace in your house. A nice fire lights the place and warms the room. However, if you let it burn out of control unchecked, it will take the house down and you with it. The point is, stress isn't something we need to fear, but we need to manage it the right ways, and actively.

⁎

A three sisters garden is a traditional garden plot that my tribe, and many tribes on the continent, grew because the three crops took care of each other. The first crop is corn, which grows tall and straight. The second crop is beans, which grow as a vine and therefore need the corn stalk as a trellis to crawl up. The third crop is squash, which weaves along the ground and will wrap tendrils around weeds and choke them out. Squash also has big leaves, which lock in moisture for all three. But the best part of this teamwork, and why we call them the "three sisters," is that what one crop takes out of the soil, the other two are putting back in. Scientists call this "symbiosis," when natural systems are stronger when they're grown together than if they were grown separately.

The key to protecting and caring for our warrior spirit in the midst of overwhelming stress so that we can fulfill our roles is to create our own three sisters garden. We can create a nurturing environment of strength, growth, and support, or we can allow ourselves to be stuck in an environment of negativity, hostility, and fear. This choice is up to us. So let's talk about how to build an environment that feeds our warrior spirit and keeps us strong in life and on our path of service. Just like the three sisters, that solid environment has three elements: what we consume, our daily habits and practices, and what we need for our support and growth.

1. What We Consume

Three decades ago, an elder told me, "Our spirits are like sponges—they soak up whatever they're around." The older I get, the more I believe it, and it's our job to make sure we're soaking up the right stuff every day. But regardless, we're all *informavores*, gluttons of information, stuffed and bloated at times, but so often anemic and starving in wisdom. Information based on fearmongering, attacks on others, or rumors leaves us angry, confused, or depleted. Ideas that inspire and clarify our path ahead, in contrast, give us hope and strengthen us. The information and ideas we consume can fuel the spirit of a warrior or of a worrier. Nourishing our warrior spirit is a continual process that requires us to feed it information and ideas to illuminate meaning in our lives, strengthen our purpose, and incorporate inspiration and learning to keep us solution-oriented *every* day. We live in a tough world. If we don't do this, we drift away from serving others and into the morass of negativity, cynicism, and pessimism that is so prevalent.

2. Our Daily Habits and Practices

Habits and practices give us good patterns and structure to our days, which can then strengthen our resilience, improve our clarity and impact, and give us the ability to "reboot" and get back onto our path when we face setbacks. Habits can be as simple as morning coffee and journaling, listening to good music, practicing your faith, daily readings that inspire you, or having a morning or end-of-day routine. It can also be anything you do to recenter yourself when you get frustrated or lose focus.

Robyn Sunday-Allen, RN, MPH (Cherokee) is the CEO of the Oklahoma City Indian Clinic, leading a staff of 330 and providing comprehensive healthcare to the area's tribal population. Especially with the pressures of her position, she understands the need to prioritize and practice her own work/life balance to fulfill her duties and serve at her best. For instance, Robyn knows that she can easily take stress home and create negative impacts for her family, so she consciously decompresses on her commute home by talking to friends and listening to uplifting music before she walks through her door. As Robyn told me, "My family deserves the best of me and not the run-down version." This improves the quality of her closest relationships, which in turn improves the quality of her support structures and her warrior spirit.

Robyn's also adamant about the habits around recharge time. She says, "We don't talk about warriors needing sleep and I'm not talking about four hours. Warriors need to rest and not feel guilty for it." When we rest, we're in a better position to serve in the best of ways, including the ones that don't require extra resources. "A smile, a helping hand, and most importantly, time or a listening ear doesn't cost a thing," Robyn told me. But we can't do that if we're grumpy from lack of sleep.

So how do we deal with the stress in our lives, especially when we feel like it's crushing us under? We self-medicate. Before you freak out, let me explain. In general society, when I say the word "medicine" it usually evokes the image of a pill because we're conditioned to see it that way. Every fifth page of a magazine is marketing some drug, and every other TV commercial is promoting another one, including ones that can cause a condition that "if it lasts more than four hours" requires an ER visit.

However, when we talk about medicine in our tribal communities, the word has a very different meaning. My people call medicine "mush-kay-kay," meaning "strength that we gather from the Earth" or from our surroundings. Everything and anything can qualify as medicine, as long as it's something that keeps us healthy in mind, body, and spirit.

Our warriors took great care of themselves, using their medicine to stay strong in every way: They used ceremony and prayer; they ate well, slept well, and took care of the health of their body, mind, and spirit. This was the reason they carried the medicine bags mentioned before, which held special, sacred items like carvings, feathers, or animal teeth, or medicines like tobacco, sage, or cedar. These things were meant to give them personal power, courage, or insight. Warriors also added strength to their medicine through tattooing, war paint, the way they fixed their hair, or special foods they ate before battle. They understood that if they didn't take care of themselves and utilize their medicine, they could not effectively fulfill their role as a warrior.

Today, this medicine can be exercise, and not just a hard grind at the gym; even a fifteen-minute walk done quickly releases endorphins that can give us a natural high for two hours. Medicine could be time with family and friends or time alone. It can be a good night of sleep, eating healthy, staying hydrated, yoga, or treating yourself to a piece of chocolate. It can be reading a good book, watching a funny movie, meditation, prayer, taking a vacation or a spa day.

One of my go-to medicines is music, one of the easiest, fastest, and free ways to elevate my mood and spirit. It might be yours as well. Music is primal and connects to something deep and ancient in all of us. Use it to your advantage. Though our ancestors may not instantly relate to the funky sounds of Earth, Wind and Fire or Bruno Mars, after a few moments I've no doubt they'd resonate with the timeless connection to rhythm and be inspired to smile, bop their heads, and shake their tailfeathers too.

LAUGHTER IS THE BEST MEDICINE

Our elders have always said that laughter is the best medicine and science is proving it to be true over and over again through studies. When we laugh or smile, we don't just "feel better," we release chemicals into our bloodstream that allow us to learn faster and get along with other people better; they boost our immunity and lower our stress hormones. And you don't need a doctor, referral, or insurance to access this medicine. Next time you're upset go to the nearest bathroom, find a mirror, and smile as wide as you can and see how long you can stay upset. I dare you to do it. But don't do this if someone is in the restroom with you. It can get weird. For both of you. Laughing is a much better way to release the negative energy stress can generate than holding it in and taking it out on the next person we interact with or dumping it on the people we love most at home. Keeping your sense of humor intact by looking for the funny in everything, watching funny movies or comedians, and surrounding yourself with funny and fun-loving people are key to keeping your sense of humor and laughter muscles strong.

Laughter and humor also make us more resilient. A case study that could prove this beyond a shadow of a doubt can be found in our Native communities. We've endured a gauntlet of horrible events including genocide, disease, displacement, indignity, and pain in all its forms. Humor in our tribal communities wasn't just an asset, it was a survival tool, and it has developed a depth, sophistication, and power that borders on transcendent. Humor allows us to maintain perspective, creates breathing room, and can lift a wounded spirit.

When Hurricane Katrina hit the Gulf Coast, I was glued to the TV since I'd spent many of my growing-up years in Biloxi, Mississippi, and still had friends there. I'd see a junior reporter doing a live story, hanging on for dear life to concrete barriers or light poles, while every manner of debris flew by. In the background, I'd see palm trees whipping around so violently they'd almost touch the ground. Storms always pass and what happens to those palm trees? Most of them are still standing because they can flex. The ones that can't bear the strain are broken. Laughter and humor give us the ability to flex in the storms and remain standing after the storms pass. Our Native nations are living proof of that truth, laughing through the pain and remaining resilient.

3. Support and Growth

Without support, we feel alone. Support can include family, friends, mentors, colleagues, coworkers, online groups, and volunteer or affinity/interest groups. We all need support because we all struggle at times and need outside answers, guidance, coaching, and the collective wisdom that comes from our "tribe"—the tribe we create for ourselves! When we stop seeking or accepting support, we paint ourselves into a corner that becomes dark and stressful pretty quickly. We're made by the Creator to be social creatures, and if we're doing our journey alone, we're doing it wrong and can get into hot water fast.

When my youngest daughter, Bella, was learning to walk, she realized that when she got scared, leaning on the curtains (or the cat) for support only seemed reliable and didn't work. But leaning on the table, wall, or her parents' legs was stable and worked well. Just as we teach our own kids to know who and what to lean on in times of trouble, we need to know the same because those trying times will happen. Guaranteed.

Because of the pressure and strain of her responsibilities, Robyn Sunday-Allen also practices leaning on extended family, friends, and colleagues and has learned that "everyone is vulnerable at times, and it isn't a sign of weakness to let your allies know that you need them."

She says that to create a supportive environment, it's vital to "surround yourself with people smarter than you and capitalize on their experience." She also acknowledges that she doesn't "do well in drama" and needs balance, so several years ago, she did an environmental audit and inventoried the people who left her feeling negative (the opposite of supportive) and removed them from her life as much as possible. She says, "If I still must do business with them, I limit that time."

When we continue learning, we feel more empowered and confident in our knowledge and abilities. We also feel less stressed and more aware about where we're going and how we'll get there. For that reason, any great environment includes activities and people that challenge us to keep learning and growing; otherwise we become bored and stagnant. Nature teaches us that there are only two states of being: We're either "green and growing" or "ripe and rotting." Now, I have good great news. I just saved a bunch of money on my car insurance. (Badum-bum-shh.)

But seriously, the great news is we get to choose which side of that fence we're on. We live in a bountiful, information-filled world with limitless opportunities to learn new things, improve what we do, and grow through it all. Whether it's reading, writing, deep conversations, trying a new activity, learning a new skill, taking classes, doing volunteer work, or watching TED Talks or YouTube videos, there are endless opportunities to keep growing. After all, we're on a journey, not a road trip where we get up to speed and then coast until we stop. In other words, there is no limit to how good we can become at what we do and who we are—and if that's the case, and it is, we should never dishonor this gift of life by settling for good enough.

The people who we sometimes need the most are not always the nicest to be around. Ever have a parent, relative, coach, boss, drill instructor, or teacher who drove you nuts but made you better? These are the people who hold us to a higher standard, who demand more of us than we think we can deliver, and who push us to reach higher ground in our lives, even when it's uncomfortable. I had many "nice" teachers in high school. I don't remember most of them. However, if I live to be a thousand years old like Yoda, I will never forget Ms. Caranna. The most evil woman to ever walk planet Earth. Or so I thought when I had her as my sophomore English teacher.

The first day of class she gave us a writing assignment, the second day we turned it in, and on the third we received our grade. I'll admit I did not put maximum effort into this paper but just enough to get a decent grade. I was shocked when she returned my paper and it looked like a mafia hit scene. She used all the ink from a red pen on my paper and finished it off with a huge C−. I was frustrated and the whole year, she and I went round and round. She pushed, pulled, corrected, demanded, and would make me rewrite papers. She drove me nuts and I was convinced her job was to make me miserable. Many years later when writing my first book, *The Tiny Warrior*, I wanted to thank the people who'd helped me get there. I got Ms. Caranna's number but was reluctant to call since she still scared the spirit out of me. The first thing I asked her was why she was so hard on me. She chuckled at that and said, "Because I knew I could be. You were scratching the surface of what you could do as a writer, and I saw it with your first assignment. And with your first book coming out, I guess I was right."

At fifteen years old, I thought Ms. Caranna was a curse in my life. As an adult, I realized she'd been the best of blessings. She got me to see things in myself that I didn't know existed, things that have transformed my life, my work, and my contribution. If we're serious about becoming our best versions of ourselves and becoming the warriors we can be, those are the people and experiences we shouldn't wait for but should run to. They lead to growth and make us sharper, smarter, more capable. And better.

_!_

In this chapter, we explored the critical importance of self-care and how romanticizing the warrior role as a person without needs gets us into trouble quickly. Remember, our warriors weren't bulletproof, and neither are we. We also examined good and bad stress, and we unpacked the three sisters garden example and showed how those elements—what we consume, our habits and practices, and what we incorporate for support and growth—are keys to our ongoing strength and fulfillment of our warrior roles. Honoring these practices strengthens us to handle what we'll explore in the next chapter: when the wolf comes.

9

What to Do When the Wolf Comes

Navigating Change, Setbacks, and Loss

Martha's life was going well. In a stable marriage of five years, she was doing well in graduate school and her family was healthy. But all at once, her husband left her for a woman he was having an affair with, walking out two days before Christmas. Then her mother was diagnosed with aggressive bilateral breast cancer. Martha was so floored, she struggled to finish the semester after missing finals due to the strain. She endured months of emotional pain from a broken heart and adjustment to a radically shifted life. One of the most crucial moments of that process happened five months later when she decided to go to the movies. Alone.

"I could not muster the courage to walk into the theater

alone," she told me. She had driven to the parking lot and burst into tears, unable to get out of the car. She finally gathered the will to walk up to the box office. Once she had the ticket, Martha felt overwhelmed walking into the theater alone. After several deep breaths, she slowly walked in and remembered the excitement, popcorn, and warm feelings of going to the movies.

Martha walked in after the movie had already started. The theater was pitch dark and her eyes hadn't adjusted. Fear consumed her and she wanted to turn back and leave, but she stood there quietly for a moment. She then started to fumble to the side of the aisle, feeling for the seats and trying to find an empty one. Fortunately, the first seat she felt was empty and she took it. She told me, "I sat there shaking and sweating, thinking how stupid I was to feel that way. But the most important thing I realized was that I did this alone and found my seat in the dark. If I could do that then I could do anything."

The whole experience of enduring the pain of loss and navigating change transformed Martha and led her to become a warrior in her world. She credits the experience with enabling her to gain a deep empathy and, as she later told me, be a "good social worker and help clients as they experience life changes, transitions, anxieties, and fears."

How Our Warriors Faced Change, Setbacks, and Loss

Change is the one guarantee we have in life that we'll experience from the moment we draw our first breath until the moment we draw our last. How we handle change defines our quality of life and determines whether we suffer defeat or enjoy victory.

I often reflect on the massive, rapid changes that our Native communities have endured the last few centuries and the obstacles that had to be overcome to survive. The Indigenous people of Turtle Island (North America) had to adjust to a whole new world forced upon them from outside forces. They were exposed to new technologies, foods, religions, and political systems, all while dealing with the loss of loved ones, and sometimes entire families, caused by new diseases, warfare, and displacement. But our Native American warriors successfully adapted through it all—they *had* to—and went from using stone tools and weapons to horses, metal weapons, and repeating rifles in no time at all.

The evolution of tools, tactics, and technologies stands out as a powerful reminder that necessity drives us to learn and adapt quickly. Our warriors knew that as the geopolitical landscape shifted with the influx of Europeans and fluid alliances with other tribes, they had to adapt quickly to fulfill their role to protect and defend their people. I'm sure, like all human beings, there was a natural resistance to the new ways, and there will always be holdouts or purists who refuse to change. But most warriors across tribal nations didn't lament or throw in the towel but rather found a way forward and leveraged the new technologies and made them their own. And they did so rapidly.

For instance, the horse was reintroduced to North America only after the Spanish arrived in the early 1500s. Within just a few generations, the Plains tribes, including the Lakota and Comanche, became some of the most accomplished and legendary horse warriors in history, rivaling even those of the Mongol Empire for their skill, tactics, and dominance. The same dynamic happened with the introduction of new weapons. I remember once in a museum seeing a Winchester rifle that belonged to a Native warrior. It was decorated with brass tacks, beadwork, and carvings. That warrior had taken a piece of modern technology and made it his own.

To highlight how fast these changes happened, think about this: There were warriors at the Battle of Little Big Horn, who fought with tomahawks and bows and arrows, who were alive to witness the birth of aviation less than thirty years later. The adaptability of our Native people ensured that we still survive today.

All these systemic, fast-paced changes tested the limits of resiliency, the ability to navigate change and survive and succeed in rapidly changing conditions. Our warriors proved to be more than up to the task and serve as a stark reminder that we can do the same.

Why Change Drives Us Crazy

So, if change is a normal, natural part of life, why does it drive us so crazy? Why are we so quick to label change as bad, a setback, a lost opportunity or failure? There are three reasons change can drive us crazy, and they all have to do with challenging human nature and mindsets.

1. WE LOVE TO BE COMFORTABLE

There is nothing most of us would rather do than snuggle on the couch with a comfy blanket, tasty snacks, and Netflix. Don't lie. In fact, I almost just stopped writing this to do it myself. Change messes with our comfort because it forces us into something *else*. But the law of nature shows us that comfort doesn't lead us to become our best. In fact, sometimes we choose comfort even when it comes at the cost of the better life we could create.

For example, when a mountain lion goes looking for food, she doesn't go for the deer that is aware and vigilant. No, she goes for the one that's wandering around casually and not paying attention.

Another example. Biosphere 2 is a really cool experiment outside of Tucson, Arizona, where scientists tried to replicate Earth's environment indoors in a fully enclosed building. In the beginning, the scientists were stumped because the trees they tried to grow would grow only to a certain height, would not bear fruit, and would fall over under their own weight.

Puzzled, they figured out that it was due to the lack of wind. Wind makes trees produce "stress wood," which girds them up and hardens them for vertical growth. Without wind, the trees were soft and weak.

The simple reality is that we don't learn much or grow when things are going well. But we learn a ton about ourselves, the people around us, and the importance of our work when we are pushed into the uncomfortable zones that change often brings. I wish it wasn't like that, but then again, I wish I looked more like Brad Pitt and less like Abraham Lincoln. It is what it is.

2. WE DON'T LIKE BEING FORCED

Think back to when you were a kid and felt "forced" to do something, even something positive, like eat your vegetables, do your homework—or stop poking your sister in the eye. What did you tend to do? You'd likely dig your heels in and resist.

Similarly, as adults we resist changes, even those for our own good, like taking care of our health or learning new things, if they feel forced. When we're told what to do, it can trigger childhood feelings of powerlessness, being bossed around, and threaten our feeling of agency. For instance, changes to our organizations, like new ways of doing business or team structures, feel thrust upon us so resistance erupts. Yet how much better spent would that time and energy be in figuring out how to incorporate and benefit from those changes? We're adults, we get to choose.

Early in my military career, I worked with a government employee named Margo who served as an administrative assistant to our team. She was known by all, liked by most, and had a reputation for being a solid teammate. However, she had the unflattering distinction of being one of the last holdouts to resist using . . . the computer. She insisted on doing reports and documents on her beloved electric typewriter and refused to use the new technology, hoping against hope that it was a passing fad.

Of course, we all know the way that went. Because of computerization, things in the organization were all moving faster, but Margo wasn't. By the time she was ordered to change, the damage was done. For months of resistance, she complained, griped, and put lots of energy and time into fighting against the change that occurred anyway. However, she also ruined her reputation, becoming known as a Luddite and a complainer, and hurt the efficiency of our team. We relied on her, and she ultimately let us all down because she was so committed to resisting an inevitable change.

3. WE ARE AFRAID

Big changes shove all of our fear, insecurity, and stress to the fore because uncertainty brings fear of the unknown and highlights our lack of control. Fear has a jam session with our most vulnerable selves and plays games with our heads, hearts, and emotions, making us feel raw and exposed like a translucent baby bird. Fear of change is normal and natural and can be countered.

Getting out of the Air Force to start my own speaking business triggered my fears like nothing ever had before. The military life was familiar and stable. I not only grew up in the Air Force but served in uniform for fourteen years, and the changes I'd be going through would be dramatic and comprehensive. The fear of the changes was pushing my buttons like a Rachmaninoff concerto. I was waking up with cold sweats in the middle of the night weeks before turning in my paperwork to separate from the military.

Of course, the questions we typically ask ourselves in moments like this haunted me over and over: What if it doesn't work out? What if I fail? What if others criticize me and tell me "I told you so"?

But I also found that fear gave me a renewed focus. I planned, read, asked questions, collaborated, coordinated, and actively worked to do all I needed to do to ensure success. I wanted to turn as many unknowns into knowns as I could. I started asking different questions: What do I want to create? What do I need to do to ensure success? Where should I seek guidance and support? And the one that got me most excited was . . . What if it *does* work? Playing on that side of the fence is much more productive and promising.

Dealing with Change:
The Six "Stays"

What can we do to navigate change more gracefully when it comes and stay on the path we've chosen? We can follow what I call the Six Stays. Here they are:

STAY PHILOSOPHICAL

I love our tribal philosophy on change. Change—whether with the seasons, weather, the activity of flora and fauna, the cycle of night and day, or the circle of life itself—isn't just a "part" of life. Change *is* life. It is an integrated, inseparable part of the whole. Because of that, change doesn't need to be cursed, reviled, or avoided as we so often do. Instead, we can use our thoughts and energy to adapt to change and make it work for us.

Another philosophy I've carried for over half of my life, I stole. From Lennon. No, not the one from Russia, the one from Liverpool who was part of the Beatles. He has a lyric that says, "There's no problem, only solutions." I love that! It's simple, practical, and memorable and it works to keep me solution-oriented through change.

If you don't have a philosophy on change, I highly recommend you get one because you'll need it for the rest of your life. I know it's a tough ask, but I'm not asking you to do the easy stuff—I'm asking you to do the stuff that works. For instance, when faced with change, instead of automatically condemning the change as "bad," start asking a better question, like "What's good about this?" It takes creativity and being open to possibility, but we can always find something good if we look hard enough.

STAY CALM

When we panic or freak out, our adrenaline kicks in and allows us to do amazing things physically. But that state does not allow us to solve problems very well. Now, you don't have to go through that experience to get some clarity in your life. Good news, right? You can create clarity with a few moments of deep breathing. Take a deep breath, hold for a count of four seconds, and breathe out slowly. That simple practice brings us back to a calm state. When we stay calm, our brains can do amazing things.

The first Native American astronaut, Commander John B. Herrington, USN, Ret., of the Chickasaw Nation, is a long-time friend of mine. He tells me that astronauts are trained to operate under high-stress environments. But in the case of Apollo 13, the stress was off the charts as their craft was failing and losing oxygen. The mission commander on the ground could tell the entire team was edging toward overwhelm and if they panicked, the men would die. The way he talked and led the mission through the challenge changed the calculus. His basic tone was "Okay, folks, I know what's wrong, but tell me what's right." That sentiment helped get everyone unstuck from the problem, calm down, and find a solution. And if you know the story, you know they put something together with cardboard, rubber tubing, and duct tape that would've put MacGyver or James Bond to shame—and got home safely.

STAY GROUNDED

Let me ask you a question. Going through the COVID-19 pandemic, did your values change? Maybe they did, and you realized clearly now what was important and what wasn't. But maybe they didn't, and your values were only deepened. Either way, as we discussed before, when we know our values—and *what* we value—everything in life becomes easier because now we know what to say yes to and what to say no to. We now have clarity in the midst of chaos and a piece of solid ground to stand on, regardless of what swirls around us. We know where to put our time, energy, and skills and where not to waste them.

Dr. Phyllis Kalifeh is the president of the Children's Forum, an organization dedicated to childhood advocacy in the state of Florida. Things for their group had been going well and they were in a comfortable place. But after a tussle with a legislative staffer, things started to go sideways. Fast. Because of a disagreement regarding a policy issue, the staffer managed to squelch and pull contracts away, negatively affecting Phyllis's budget. Rather than throw in the towel, she and her team huddled up and bonded in their newfound discomfort, deciding to lean in hard on their values and cultural strengths of excellence and believing that those they served—the children, teachers, and other customers—deserved respect, value, support, and the very best they could deliver.

Phyllis and her team made efforts to grow through this moment—not just get through it. They came up with a new business plan, changed their market focus, and made hard pivots to increase opportunities to serve even better. They secured a federal grant that put them in the respected role of researchers, opening a whole new world of influencers and supporters. What they came up with was a radically different strategy for a nonprofit and not only did it work, but they've also grown substantially stronger because of it. They didn't choose the uncomfortable situation thrust upon them by the vengeful staffer, but stayed grounded and leveraged it into something better. *Much* better.

STAY FOCUSED

Especially in times of change, it's important to stay focused on what truly matters and what is important. If we get scattered and try to focus on *everything*, we're really focused on *nothing*. Again, we don't want to divide and conquer ourselves. When we stay focused on our values, what we value, and our most important goals, we know what to say yes to and what to say no to (or at least "not now"). If we see our time, energy, and decisions each day as arrows, we have only a certain number to shoot each day. Either we send them toward specific targets or we shoot in every direction and hope for something good to happen.

Let's look at it another way. If you stood out in the sunshine for five minutes, what would happen to you? You'd feel warm, relaxed. Even though there's a star only 93 million miles away from Earth, next-door neighbors in space terms, pumping an insane amount of energy at this place, it's spread out. It doesn't have a significant effect on any one place, including you. However, if you harness that same energy that's falling gently on your face into a magnifying glass, you get a whole different experience. Any ten-year-old kid can tell you what you can do with that. (This ex-ten-year-old kid used to do it all the time and I got busted for it. You can light your backyard on fire. It's awesome!)

It all comes down to focused energy. Focus on the right things and you get the right results. Focus on *everything* and you get none.

STAY FLEXIBLE

When things change, we must exercise our creativity and activate our warrior spirit to find a way forward and overcome the obstacles. We've all heard the adage, "There's more than one way to skin a cat." (Yes, it's a terrible saying. I don't know why you'd ever want to skin a cat, but if you did—and please don't—know that there's more than one way to do it!) The takeaway here is that we need to stay open and flexible in moving forward to get to our goals. Our goals and strategy (the "what") may remain the same in times of change, but sometimes the tactics we use (the "how") can change—and sometimes must.

What does water do, when it comes down a mountain, with all its fury and potential, and runs into a rock? Slam on the brakes and say, "Aw, who put that there? Back up, back up . . ." No, of course not. It goes over it. And if it can't do that? It goes around it. And if it can't do that? It goes under it. And if it can't do that? It knocks it out of the way or goes through it. That why we have rivers and corresponding canyons all over the world. Water finds a way to flow to its goals and so must we. Stay flexible.

STAY CONNECTED

A common philosophy in our Native cultures is that we are all connected. Inside the circle of life is one big, inextricable web connecting everything to everything. The Lakota say "mitakuye oyasin"—"to all my relations." That doesn't mean just your kids or your grandma, it's everyone. Use your connections to draw strength. As mentioned before, we need each other and we're better when we're with the right people.

Our warriors *never* fought alone for the same reasons, so don't feel the need or necessity to struggle on your own either. We all need support; we all need outside answers, encouragement, and connection to others. We're stronger, smarter, more empathetic, courageous, and resilient in that environment.

Dealing with Setbacks

We all deal with setbacks where things don't go according to plan, we're thrown a curveball, or we lose resources, personnel, or support or waste money or time on an effort. And the question isn't *if* they appear, but *when* they do. The part-time philosopher and ex–heavyweight boxing champ of the world Mike Tyson said, "Everyone has a plan until they get punched in the mouth." How many times have we experienced that in our own lives and careers?

I read a May 2011 article in *National Geographic* called "The Coming Storm," about a group of people in Bangladesh who live on the floodplains created by three major rivers. These people inhabit countless small islands that appear for a time, disappear, and then reappear somewhere else based on rainfall, floods, the tides, etc. Despite this ever-changing lifestyle of setback upon setback, the families raise crops and kids and build a successful life on these islands called "chars." The article stated that to live a life like this is like "winning an Olympic medal in adaptation."

One of the men interviewed had moved once a year for his whole life—and he's sixty! But he's also raised seven kids who "never missed a meal." The houses can be disassembled and reassembled quickly; the family's bags are always neatly packed next to their beds for a quick move. The man said, "No matter how much we worry, the end is all the same." He says the real secret is "not to think too much." Despite living in a tough and dynamic environment, these people thrive. In their world, setbacks are a way of life. What can we learn from them?

GO WITH THE FLOW

Instead of constantly worrying about things to come or getting hung up on setbacks, the char people literally go with the flow. They farm an island for as long as they can and when the river washes it away, they find a new one to farm. They don't curse God, deplore the economy, get an ulcer from worry, bemoan their existence, or complain about their fate—they simply go with the flow.

EXPECT IT

The char people are always prepared for the setbacks they *know* will come. They don't hope, wish, want, wait, or live, in fear. Instead, they keep their possessions in order, ready to move when they must, and most importantly they have a mindset that is ready too. This is the key to resilience—having a mindset that not only is prepared for setbacks but *expects* it. When it arrives, you are ready to succeed.

DON'T THINK TOO MUCH

The char people feel that the situation concerning the ever-changing river "is what it is." They don't overanalyze, complicate, or assess the situation in painful detail as we may do. If we're faced with a situation we can't change, such as a dictator boss, tough economy, pandemic, or loss of a loved one, we also see—*it is what it is.* The char people survive and thrive in these moments because of this: When it is what it is, they *do what they must do.* They can't change the river or its flow, but they can take action to keep succeeding in an extremely difficult environment.

The char people of Bangladesh may be the most resilient people in the world because they have happily lived, for generations, in one of the most unforgiving and varied environments in the world. They thrive in those tough conditions because they know the secrets to resiliency through setbacks— and now you do too.

Remember those little egg-shaped toys called Weebles? I was a huge fan, had all the Weebles swag, the airplane, the treehouse. They had a jingle that said, "Weebles wobble, but they don't fall down." I love that. And it's a dynamic we can create when we use all these strategies mentioned above to handle setbacks and when we build the right environment around us (discussed in the last chapter). We're able to handle whatever life presents more gracefully and successfully.

Dealing with Loss: When the Wolf Comes

But what happens when you receive a devastating blow in your life, one that knocks the wind out of you and breaks your heart? Or your will to go on? Those dark, scary, and painful moments are the wolf coming to call at your door. This is the moment when everything you know, everything you are, is tested. This is the moment when your warrior spirit is crucial.

September 21, 2003. I had just returned home to Colorado from a busy eight-day trip to Minnesota and drifted off into a deep sleep. My wife at the time, Arienne, was pregnant with our second child and was out in California visiting her family with our daughter, Gabrielle. At six in the morning, I got a panicked call from Arienne. "I'm having contractions. They hurt." I could hear the concern in her voice and felt my blood run cold. She was six months pregnant. It was way too early to have contractions—something was wrong. I was on the next flight.

Due to an abrupted placenta, Arienne started labor early and our son, Kieran, was delivered by emergency C-section three months early. He was two pounds, seven ounces but stable and so our fear turned to cautious hope. When I first saw him in his crib, he was a little boy at the bottom of a tangle of tubes, wires, and beeping monitors. So tiny, but a head covered with chocolate-brown cornsilk hair with a perfect nose and big feet. He was beautiful. We spent hours at his bedside singing and talking to him. We placed an eagle plume above his crib, given to us by friends Keith and Jackie Anna. We prayed—hard.

On the third day, our hope was shattered when the doctors told us Kieran had developed a severe bleed on the brain. He was already on a ventilator. All the dreams we'd imagined of going fishing, playing catch, or reading bedtime stories with

Kieran were in jeopardy. I kissed his hands, head, legs, feet, and every part of his tiny body that didn't have tape or a tube. More prayers and tears, and the painful reality set in that our beautiful boy may not be coming home with us.

All was right in the world the day they allowed us to hold him. I cried tears of joy and thanked the Creator for this little boy, this spirit of light. On the seventh and last night of his struggle, in the arms of his mom and dad, Kieran Cruz Vanas passed from this world into the next. We never got to hear him cry, or laugh, or see him play. It was the saddest day of my life.

We were heartbroken, and I felt that my life had shattered into a thousand pieces. I was determined to not lose anything else—my family, my friends, my joy for life—after losing our son. I was using everything I had in me to stay strong, focus on the good, and maintain my balance. But I was struggling. My pride kept me locked in a prison of my own creation and I resisted opening to other possibilities of help and support. I felt like an impostor if I needed to get outside help since I was in the profession of showing others how to be strong. Yet I felt I was falling apart. On my worst days, I stood on the edge of a dark abyss and wanted to jump in. I was angry and depressed, and felt robbed and scared, worried about the next thing we'd lose. It's a terrible feeling to approach life from the perspective where you're no longer playing to win, but playing just to not lose the next thing.

One month after Kieran's passing, I traveled to Hannahville Indian Community in the Upper Peninsula of my home state of Michigan. I was nervous to be working again and not sure how I'd handle it. Would I break down or fall apart? Thankfully, the community knew about our circumstances and was wonderful, showering me with loving support and the traditional honor of gifting me a blanket. Even more, they asked if I'd be willing to go through a "wiping of the tears" ceremony for me with Earl Meshigaud, a Potawatomi elder and healer. I was loath to admit it, but I knew I'd been struggling and needed help. I said yes.

The "wiping of the tears" ceremony is meant to release the pain of loss and negative energy that builds up in us after a heartbreak. In the ceremony, we humbly ask for help from our ancestors and those who have passed on before us. I sat in Earl's rustic home surrounded by the swirls of tangy smoke from burning sweetgrass and cedar as he gently tapped me with an eagle wing fan. It was an intimate ceremony with just us two and his helper. The only light was from burning wood in the fireplace. I could feel, as much as hear, his low raspy voice leading me to do something I was so afraid to do: fully embrace the pain of my loss. He guided me on a journey, to deeply explore and reflect on the loss and release the pain of it. He gave me a medicine bag for healing, meant only for me, as a spiritual balm for my wounds and to reflect on my blessings.

The ceremony was a pivotal moment in my healing process. I cried like I've never cried before. I felt like walls of resistance had melted away through the tears; I felt unstuck, and was better able to choose how I wanted to move forward. In fact, that opened me up to finally agree to get grief counseling, which my wife recommended we do together but I had resisted, seeing it as a surrender or defeat.

It was a surrender. But it was not a defeat.

The key factor in dealing with a painful loss is to acknowledge the pain and face the wolf. Otherwise, we can be consumed by it. Not acknowledging our emotions leaves us scrambling to suppress them, minimize them, or deny they even exist. Trying to outrun our reality just leaves us tired out, and not processing our emotions leaves us emotionally constipated. And stuck. The truth is, unresolved emotions will emerge again eventually, sometimes in unhealthy or toxic ways.

Until the ceremony, I didn't realize that it takes more courage to be open to others when we're in pain than it does to hold it hidden inside. Sometimes the strongest, most courageous act of a warrior is to ask someone else for help when we feel stuck, scared, or defeated, because it requires vulnerability, humility, and overcoming our ego. In exchange, we get unstuck, begin healing, and can start moving forward again.

When the wolf comes, we need the humility to know that a universal connector is pain. We've all experienced pain of loss, and we needn't isolate ourselves when it happens to us. I credit my healing journey to friends, family, elders, counselors, and, thankfully, having a positive, supportive environment around me. I'm grateful I'd developed basic skills and self-care practices in my life that gave me resiliency and kept me thinking long-term.

In the precious moments my wife and I had with Kieran,

he reminded us that life is a sacred gift and it's worth living to the fullest, no matter the length of time. Despite all the obstacles our son faced, he desperately fought to live until his last breath. He didn't quit or give up. Life goes on and I've tried to stay focused on the countless blessings we all have, such as family, friends, and our own lives. Going through an experience like this can bring bitterness or wisdom and I want to live to honor Kieran, believing that happiness is found in cherishing the memories of him and living for now, not becoming angry or resentful of what's been lost.

I also learned to treasure our gifts and loved ones like there is no tomorrow because eventually, there won't be—and that moment always comes too soon. My hope is that when you finish reading this, you'll hug your loved ones, kiss your kids, or call a friend you cherish. In our busy world, it's easy to forget that our greatest treasures can be under our own roof. Take the time to honor and love those special gifts in your life while you can.

THE TRANSFORMATION OF CEREMONY

Many of our traditional tribal ceremonies require sacrifice, deprivation, and isolation and some involve pain, fear, and exhaustion because they're intended to *pull us* into the spiritual world where deep, lasting changes can occur. As I mentioned before, going without food, water, and shelter for four days and nights was extremely difficult during my four years of the vision quest. Enduring the rigors of the Sun Dance, dancing barefoot from sunrise to sunset each day and then piercing our chests with buffalo bone skewers, was scary and painful and humbled me to my knees in tears. These elements may seem cruel to those outside our tribal communities, but they offered blessings that changed my life. They were deeply transformative. Ceremony requires us to surrender, for a time, our own pride, ego, food, shelter, comfort, relationships, and familiarity in exchange for insight, perspective, growth, and wisdom. What we come away with is always different from how we arrived. Who we are when we exit a ceremony is also different.

The Changes We Don't Choose

We know life is a humbling trip . . . but c'mon, man! Just when we think we've got it all figured out, the cards get reshuffled—or the table is overturned, and the place gets set on fire. Through the recent anxieties of the pandemic, political, social, and economic turmoil, or suddenly finding yourself as your kid's homeroom teacher in addition to holding on to your job virtually, things have been hard to say the least. And even worse if we lost relatives or friends, including to COVID-19, and couldn't attend to them or their funerals at the end. I know this has left us shaken . . . and to think, it all started with worrying about toilet paper.

But changes can trigger growth, open opportunities, and make us better than before. The cold truth is we don't learn much when the sky is blue, all is well, and we're comfortable.

But we are often transformed in deep, meaningful ways through painful change and can grow tremendously. We wouldn't *choose* these changes, but they're here. Our warrior spirit is being tested and lately that test is like taking the SATs while running the Tough Mudder. Sir Winston Churchill said, "Never let a good crisis go to waste" as a reminder to make sure to gather the wisdom, lessons, and opportunities that show up. And they do.

Even the most heartbreaking changes push us to assess where we are on the journey, as well as where we're going, and spark new awareness in our choices. Change gives us the chance to pause and examine the tools we have and identify the ones we need. Change reminds us of who our friends really are and who was posing as one. Change also spurs us to take inventory of our skills and talents and recommit to moving forward. Perhaps most important, change often moves us to reaffirm what's truly important and worthy of our time and effort—and to dump what's frivolous, petty, or wasteful.

The changes we don't choose will test us, sometimes in harsh, unexpected ways. We wouldn't wish some of the changes we've endured on our enemies, but they've come, nonetheless. What we come away with will be up to us. We don't choose all the changes that happen to us, but we do get to choose *who* we are and *how* we are as we move through them.

Will you leverage your tough times into a reminder of your resilience or cast them aside as annoyance? Can this be something to *grow* through and not just *get* through? Will you accept the wisdom this part of the journey is offering—or will you walk away in anger over having gone through it?

These moments are humbling, and we don't have to have all the answers in that moment, but they also remind us that we can tap our warrior spirit and make change work for us. We just need to keep putting one foot in front of the other and do the next right thing. We can ask, "What is this moment teaching me?" and "What have I learned through this?" This rebirth of awareness leads us to better choices so we can forge a better path ahead—not because we're hoping, wishing, or praying for it—but because we are *deciding to make it so* by making these changes work for us. On its face, change isn't good or bad, it's the natural order of the universe. It's what we do in those moments of change that define it for us.

> If the Great Spirit wanted men to stay in one place, he would have made the world stand still; but he made it to always change, so birds and animals can move and always have green grass and ripe berries, sunlight to work and play, and night to sleep; summer for flowers to bloom, and winter for them to sleep; always changing. Everything for good; nothing for nothing.
>
> —CHIEF FLYING HAWK (OGLALA LAKOTA)

10

Transform into an Elder

Warriors Don't Retire

A few years ago, I was traveling down Highway 13 along Lake Superior in northern Wisconsin into the community of the Red Cliff Band of Lake Superior Chippewa. Along the highway, nowhere near town, I saw a small grandma with snow-white hair trudging along with purpose, almost marching. I slowed down, thinking she might be lost or need help. She looked up and shone with the confidence of a warrior with purpose. We nodded to each other as a greeting and, seeing she was okay, I continued, not realizing I was witnessing a long-held ritual.

After reaching my hotel room later that evening, I turned on the TV and saw a state-sponsored program that honored citizens making a difference. One of the honorees featured was a small grandma with snow-white, curly hair and a childlike twinkle in her eyes—it was the same elder I'd seen on the roadside! She was known as Grandma Genny in her community of Red Cliff and was a legend in her own time.

The next day, I spoke at a community program and was honored with an unexpected gift: I got to meet Genevieve Goslin, aka Grandma Genny. This wonderful woman was truly a leader by example: part grandma, part artist, part warrior, part teacher, and all heart. Born in 1920, she was Ojibwe. Her Ojibwe names were Waabijiig'kwe (White Crane Woman) and Migizi Ogimaakwe (Head Eagle Woman). She struggled as a single mother after her husband passed away and deferred her dream of pursuing higher education to raise her family. She finally went back to school, fighting to set a good example for her family and community, and at age sixty-three, she attended the Institute of American Indian Arts (IAIA) and earned her associate of arts degree with a 4.0 grade point average. She then used these skills to teach others in her community traditional crafts like weaving, beading, moccasin making, and drawing.

Grandma Genny also served as a foster grandmother, worked with students from Head Start to college, and taught Native American history and language to students in elementary through high school. At eighty-eight years old, she was given the Wisconsin Friend of Education Award for her significant contributions to education and her lifelong love of education and passing that along to the children of her community. The previous year, she was honored for her outstanding service to education by the Bayfield School District.

Grandma Genny is an example of a lifelong warrior who becomes an elder and lives out the belief that it's never too late to follow your dreams. She is the kind of elder we should all aim to be because she was:

Focused—Grandma Genny looked at life as a gift, focusing on the good in the world around her, what she was grateful for, and the abilities she had to work with each day. She kept a weather eye on what she most wanted to be and worked her whole life to realize it, going back to school years later to get her education and sharing everything she learned with her community. Grandma Genny was a trailblazer as a Native and a single mother and showed a lifetime's tenacity in her goal of developing herself to better serve her people. She stayed focused and never quit, inspiring others with her example that it's never too late to fulfill a dream.

Fit—Years ago, a doctor told Grandma Genny that she had a condition that would cause her pain for the rest of her life. True to form, she refused to accept defeat in the diagnosis and instead went outside to walk. Each day, she walked farther. At the end of the month, she had no more pain and would walk one mile every day since, rain or shine (hence why I spotted her along the highway). Grandma Genny understood that when it comes to our bodies, you either "use it or lose it," and that activity of any kind, at any level, is truly medicine to our bodies. When I met her, she was eighty-seven years young, full of life and energy. Her vigor and stamina weren't due to luck—they were acts of sheer will, carried out each day along the shores and roads along Lake Superior.

Free—Though Grandma Genny had many victories, she also dealt with racism, the death of loved ones, poverty, illness, and so much more. However, you could tell by her radiant energy and constant smile that she walked lightly in this world, unburdened by carrying the baggage of pain, regret, or anger that so many of us carry. She was free of these by choice—and free to enjoy the blessings life offers each day. This is what true wisdom really is in the end.

Fun—Because she stayed focused, fit, and free, Grandma Genny was a fun person to be around. During my community program, she was my anchor. I would look out into the crowd and feel delighted as I watched her smile, laugh, poke the person next to her, nod her head in agreement, and do all the things that encourage you when you speak in front of others. She glowed in her brightly colored floral shirt and seemed to be one of those special spirits that realizes life is too good to miss. She led by example, not telling us how to live our precious lives, but showing us how.

At the end of the program, I signed a book for Grandma Genny with a heartfelt inscription. She looked at it, smiled widely, and leaned over the table, put her hand around my neck, and kissed my cheek. She sent my spirit soaring to the clouds and my smile stretched ear to ear. I lost both sets of my grandparents many years ago but found that familiar warmth and connection with Grandma Genny. She was a grandma to the whole Red Cliff community—and for that day, she was mine too.

Becoming an Elder

Our tribal warriors never retired, but they did change roles as they matured and were no longer able to fight and protect as they once could. Ultimately our best warriors evolved into our tribes' best elders, sharing the lifetime of experience, lessons, and stories with others. Elders were, and still are, the backbone of our tribal communities. Generosity and giving back were also central tribal values.

Everyone in the tribe had a role and responsibility to develop in order to contribute, from the youngest to the eldest. Even children learned basic helping skills to assist around the village, from collecting firewood to helping elders. When it was time to go out hunting, our warriors provided nourishment to the people and made it a practice to share the first kill with everyone to honor those values. Our warriors also served and contributed by being protectors and fighting when necessary. Our elders do the same by contributing a lifetime of knowledge and wisdom to those in their tribe. In fact, in many of our tribes, the real measure of wealth wasn't how much you had but how much you could give away, and the best elders I've ever met live by that credo.

Warriors evolved into elders purposefully by collecting as many stories, as many lessons, and as much experience, knowledge, and wisdom as they possibly could on their journey. They collected all this not to hoard it, show off, or use it to control others (several of those I interviewed relayed stories of watching that destructive process of knowledge hoarding or using information as a control tool in an organization). They collected all this to then fulfill the elder role, by sharing and empowering others in their tribe with what they had gathered, so everyone around them benefited. This is also the difference between becoming an elder—and just getting older.

Getting older is automatic, and none of us can stop the hands of time (though we do try, don't we?). I look back at how much my life and body have changed through the years. For instance, I remember shopping for cereal with my mom when I was a kid. Remember back in the day when they used to put toys in the cereal box? Well, I couldn't have cared less what was in the box of cereal, it could have been cat kibble—I just wanted the toy. Yet, once we hit forty-five years old, what's the number one ingredient we look for in cereal? Fiber. What a sad turn of events.

The truth is, getting older is automatic—but getting better is not. Getting better is by design. Keep growing, keep learning (like we covered in chapter 7)—and keep sharing. When you do, you'll be fulfilling the role of an elder and the world needs that now more than ever.

People can lose hope when they don't have reminders that things truly can get and be better. As elders, we can be that reminder and display our warrior spirit at work when we stay positive, show resilience, and continue to be a coach, friend, and encourager-in-chief to those we lead and serve. That outward display of cynicism or apathy sometimes shown by others may be because it's been so long since they have seen a positive attitude, a resilient mindset, or a respectful demeanor that they've forgotten what it looks like. Be the example.

Embrace It All So You Can Share It All

Our elders passed on knowledge, wisdom, values, and traditions down through the centuries through the power of story. So it's no surprise that we read books and watch movies the way we do because we are conditioned from ancient times to be fascinated by good, compelling stories. They are the things that stick to our mental ribs. Think of your favorite movies. Whether you picked *It's a Wonderful Life*, *Avatar*, or *Finding Nemo*, think of the story arc and what the characters endure. They have struggles, ups, downs, self-doubt, disasters, and moments where everything almost fails. But they find something deeper inside, leverage their strength or ideas, and come through victorious in the end. This is why we watch these movies! Yet, when the same dynamics of the stress and strain, the ups and downs, and the struggles in our life happen, we think life is unfair or the world is out to get us. Embrace everything you encounter. Be proud of the struggles you've endured, the fears you've faced, and the mistakes you've made that served as lessons. You are creating your own epic action-adventure, rom-com, sci-fi, thriller, dramatic biopic in your life each day and it's going to be a blast to share all this with others someday.

Imagine this movie plotline: *A girl is born in a small town . . . She grows up, finishes school, and gets a job she doesn't like . . . She does the job for forty years . . . Then she dies.* No one is going to watch that movie! When you're older, grayer, and sitting in a rocking chair on a porch, all your kids, grandkids, and great-grandkids fanned out on the ground all around you, my wish for you is that you have the best stories to share about adventure, love, passionate pursuits, fears faced head-on, heartbreak, euphoric joy, stumbles, victories, and everything in between. No one wants to be in that chair, with eager eyes fixed on you, waiting for the stories and wisdom to issue forth, and you rock back and forth and say, "I got nothin'!" Embrace it all. You are an elder in the making, storing up the wisdom you're gaining with each year that you'll be able to share with your tribe.

We can also play a vital role in creating positive change by actively sharing our stories with others—in person, in print, and online. Sharing our successes, failures, the wisdom gained through struggles, the fears overcome, and the thrill of accomplishing big goals can inspire and impress upon others what they can do for themselves and those they serve. Our oral traditions taught lessons, values, and virtues and worked the same way by inspiring others to change, to live right, and to succeed, through the power of stories. We can lead by example and play a critical role in providing what is often in short supply across our communities: hope. We can make things better and it can start with us when we share our stories to illuminate someone else's path.

MAKE TIME FOR STORY TIME

We all know how powerful stories are in our lives, and our Indigenous communities relied on them solely since most didn't have any form of written language. Stories stick to the ribs and inspire our minds. However, we're all busy people in a busy world, and the informational exchange that happened through beautiful stories told around a village fire are long gone. But we can intentionally carve space into our schedules to share stories and to receive them from others. Creating a story exchange through one-on-one meetups with mentors and mentees, a company spotlight in the newsletter on someone willing to share a story-based lesson, or doing rotating story time at the beginning of meetings can all be value-added activities. We accelerate our learning curve when we hear these stories, and we clarify our own valuable learning when we share ours with others. Every person I interviewed for this book was a hands-down, passionate believer in the value of story and all acknowledged the deep, positive impact stories have had in their own development.

PASS THE TORCH AND LIGHT ANOTHER FIRE

Anyone who has achieved greatly in their service to others undoubtedly had someone who provided support, guidance, and the priceless gift of encouragement. When someone sees our potential, it ignites a self-belief that is hard to quantify. But I do know from personal experience that it has a huge impact in our trajectory. And I'm willing to bet you'd agree. Simply taking someone aside to give some simple encouragement, a bit of genuine praise, can make a world of difference in that person's development and launch our spirit through the clouds.

Herb Clah Jr. (Navajo) is the HR director for the Utah Navajo Health System, located in the Four Corners area and serving the region's Indigenous populations, primarily those of the Navajo Nation. He credits a caring elder for his service journey and development into the high-responsibility roles he fulfills today. He says, "Early in my career, a gentleman named Max took me under his wing. His biggest contribution in my development was his confidence and trust that allowed me to make my own decisions and allowed me to make mistakes without fear of reprisal." In fact, I heard this time and time again from those I interviewed, that our mentors are critical to nurturing not just our skill sets but more importantly, our confidence in our own abilities. Herb continued, "Max would counsel me and offer his wisdom in how to handle people. He showed me respect, care, and taught me humility."

I can relate to Herb's example and have one of my own to share. My first boss was a wonderful mentor and taught me as much about myself as he did about my job. He had high expectations for those of us on his team, gave me leeway to learn without being punitive in corrections, and gave me a heavy dose of encouragement, which was priceless. I was a freshly minted officer, a brand-new second lieutenant. Major Donnell Smith was an Air Force Academy graduate and an F-15 pilot. Obviously he was, as the late Stuart Scott of ESPN would say, "cooler than the backside of a pillow," but Major Smith was also smart, kind, patient, and compassionate. I looked up to him from the beginning. Being African American, he personally understood the value of good mentorship and leveraging it to face and defeat stereotypes, stiff odds, and prejudice.

I remember the first one-on-one mentorship moment with him. I was in the middle of planning a complicated recruiting trip with many moving parts and lots of coordination. I walked into his office and laid out a laundry list of concerns, details, and questions. I hadn't gotten very far down the list, figuratively wringing my hands, and asked what I should do. Major Smith seized the moment and sat up in his chair, smiled, and simply said, "I don't know, Lieutenant Vanas. What do *you* think you should do?" Coming from a very regimented experience at the Academy, this was a breath of fresh air that was intoxicating to me. To be reminded that I could (and was expected to) make my own decisions about how I executed my part of our mission was liberating and exciting. The whole year, he taught me skills, shared wisdom, laid out expectations, and provided lots of encouragement. I was so grateful to him for taking the time he did to teach me to be innovative, bold, and committed to my decision-making process. It created a positive impact and confidence I'm still benefiting from today.

DON'T SHY AWAY FROM THE PAIN—IT CAN BE YOUR BEST STUFF

Manoomin, or wild rice, is a timeless food staple of the Indigenous peoples around the Great Lakes, including the Anishinaabe people, the Ojibwe, the Potawatomi, and my tribe, the Ottawa. This superfood must be processed to remove the hull and reveal the versatile, edible grains of rice (technically, wild rice is actually a grass, but I digress).

Our own stories can be the same when we discount or dismiss their value and leave them encased in a hull of resistance, anger, shame, embarrassment, pain, or fear of stirring up the past. If we have that much emotional energy about our past stories, then they're worth revisiting to process those emotions, and feel the feelings, so we're not imprisoned by them. And once we get through that hull, we can mine the treasure trove of lessons gifted to us by those experiences. When we look at the hard, painful stuff we've gone through, we see real-world examples of resiliency, grit, creative problem-solving, healing, and dealing with adversity that hold priceless wisdom for us and can be shared to nourish others in our tribe.

I've had many conversations over the years about this idea. One woman I spoke with had a daughter in high school and wanted to talk to her daughter about going to college but felt hesitant to do so. She explained that she was a high school dropout and felt it would be hypocritical to promote higher education with her daughter. A man I spoke with had a similar issue with guiding his son to stay out of trouble. The man had been incarcerated and had struggled with substance use. The shame of his past formed a barrier between him and his ability to parent his son in the way he wanted. What neither realized was that they weren't coming from a deficit in their wisdom, they were coming from the high ground of credibility and firsthand experience! The woman *knew* the struggles of making it in the world without education and the man *knew* the consequences of bad choices. They didn't read it, they lived it.

We're all works in progress. While it's great to share success stories, the lessons we learned when we struggled, fell short, or failed can be even more powerful in their impact on others. It requires vulnerability and authenticity and can form a deep, engaged connection to those with whom you share your stories. The elders and mentors in my life who made the most impact weren't the ones who shared only how to do things right, but those who shared what they learned when things went terribly wrong.

I've had countless elders in our tribal communities that have guided, shaped, corrected, coached, and encouraged me to be where I am and who I am on my journey. They showed me how to be the kind of elder I want to be with their examples. They gave their knowledge willingly but not insistently— it was there for the asking, but they didn't preach, lecture, or browbeat. They shared their treasure troves of humanity, life experience, cultural teachings, and wisdom. They were real, authentic, and direct and didn't sugarcoat the sour patches of life. Yet all of them shared a warm, inviting sense of humor and humility, which is critical in forming a trusting relationship and enabling those elders to have influence and impact on others. Some of these elders include Selo Black Crow (Lakota), John Chaske and Melvin Grey Bear (both Spirit Lake Sioux Tribe), Bea Shawanda (Ottawa/Potawatomi), Rick Williams (Lakota), Phil Hunter (Tule River Tribe), Keith Anna (Delaware/Choctaw), Commander John B. Herrington, USN, Ret. (Chickasaw), Dr. John Molina (Yavapai Apache /Yaqui), Larry Blacksmith (Lakota), Henrietta Mann (Cheyenne), Austin Box (Southern Ute), Dr. Cornel Pewewardy (Comanche-Kiowa), Norbert Hill (Oneida), and my own grandmother, Gladys Vanas (Ottawa). This list is nowhere close to complete, but the influence of all these elders reverberates in my spirit and actions daily.

Mentoring the Way Nature Intended

A good elder was a skilled mentor in order to actively facilitate learning for others. Our tribal cultures were master observers, taking in massive amounts of vital information from nature on how to leverage their own resources, live a good life, build community, and raise their children. Whether in mountain lions teaching their cubs to hunt, deer showing their fawns how to stay stealthy, or hawks mentoring their chicks to fledge and fly, the power of mentorship was everywhere in nature. Learning by watching the way animals and birds mentored their young, Native peoples saw the value in the practice and replicated it in their tribes. From the earliest age and at every stage of development, Native peoples were mentored by others. Everyone had a role to learn, and everyone served as a mentor and teacher to someone else. The survival of the tribe depended on this mentorship process. If little boys didn't learn how to hunt, the tribe could starve. If little girls weren't shown how to sew moccasins, the hunters couldn't effectively hunt. If warriors didn't teach the skills needed in warfare, the tribe could fall prey to enemies. And if elders didn't mentor others in their wisdom, the tribe would have poor leadership and a lack of harmony. Everyone depended on everyone else and in our organizations today, the same dynamic is often at work too, but we don't recognize it until we see problems.

By the way, mentorship is not "watch what I do and do it." Real, active mentorship is "come over here and let's do this together." Through that process, not only are the motions and actions reproducible, but the conversations about them are vital as well. Whether it's teaching someone to drive, showing them how to do an end-of-shift report, or developing their leadership skills, active mentorship ensures the clear transmission of accurate information, builds confidence, and fosters new skill sets.

For example, I remember being an elementary-school-age

kid, maybe ten, down at the docks on the Gulf Coast of Mississippi. I was fascinated watching the older fishermen throwing out and then pulling in their casting nets, dumping their catch onto the docks. An elderly man saw my interest and asked if I wanted to learn how to do it. He didn't just say "watch me," he guided me as I held the net, helped me bunch the wet netting over my arm and hold the outer rope ring with my teeth (the way real fishermen did it) so I could cast it out. He also showed me how to pull it in quickly and then properly release the catch on the dock. It was a moment when it was no longer something other people did, it was something I could do too. After that, I saved up money and bought an eight-foot casting net of my own that I used for the next several years.

Of course, mentorship is not always about teaching skills. Sometimes it's about exemplifying a mindset. Introduced to you earlier, Robyn Sunday-Allen shared a moving testament to the wise elders and caring mentors who are able to instill a mentality that can leave a legacy of good in our lives. She says, "We recently lost a worker who was ninety years old. She worked until she was eighty-six and hardly ever missed a day of work. She would always say that she didn't like it when younger people would say 'I wish it were Friday' or they were 'just trying to get through the day.' She taught me to stay in the moment and be thankful for the here and now." Perhaps learning the mentality that reminds us of the joy of life and service itself is the most valuable thing we can inherit from our elders and mentors. Robyn agrees and believes that "being a warrior means that we develop others," and that starts with mentoring the right mindset.

CIRCULAR MENTORSHIP

At every stage of our lives and careers, we benefit from being mentors to others and being mentored by others. It's a beautiful exchange of information, a good trade, that benefits everyone involved. We learn new perspectives and skills when we're mentored and learn much more about our own skill sets and development when we teach what we know to others. And don't overlook the fact that we can benefit tremendously by having a mentor who is younger than us. Yes, it takes humility to be willing to continue learning from others. But a game-changing edge in our development can be found when we're willing to learn from those younger employees and teammates.

Too often we let tradition, pride, or ego get in the way of staying humble enough to access what younger generations are bringing to the collective table and allowing them to teach us. Many of those I interviewed are leveraging this potent source of knowledge and benefiting tremendously. I've personally been mentored by people much younger than me in everything from technology to social media, and from diversity to social justice movements. I've been blown away by some of the creative approaches and fresh insights our up-and-coming warriors are contributing to the world. I've found it fun and fascinating to trade ideas with others from different ages, backgrounds, beliefs, and experience levels. Gather the good information and wisdom wherever you may find it. Remember, the goal is to continually learn and improve so we can continue contributing to our own tribes, whether that be family, team, clients, customers, company, campus, country, or planet.

In her role as education director, Joyce McFarland is a warrior for her Nez Perce Tribe, the people of that icon of courageous leadership, Chief Joseph. She told me she has a book in progress that says: *If you want wisdom, speak to the elders. If you want the truth, listen to the children.* She believes it may have been attributed to the Lakota Tribe. With thirty years of experience working for her tribe, mainly in youth and education programs, she's seen this insight proven to be true, over and over again.

One example she shared is where a young person gave the best, most logical answer to solve a long-standing question they had in their tribal Education Department. They wondered why they consistently had a two-to-one female-to-male ratio for tribal scholarship recipients. Joyce often talked to other adults to try to figure out why more tribal females were going to college than the tribe's males, which was a national trend as well. After trying to understand this dynamic, she got the best insight from a girl who attended one of their tribal youth advisory board meetings.

"After explaining the two-to-one female-to-male ratio for tribal members in college," Joyce told me, "she offered a possible reason. She said that girls think they need a college education to get a good job while boys think they can get a good job right out of high school. It was so profound to me, but to her she thought it was an easy explanation." The following year, Joyce was attending a conference where a speaker was discussing college accession rates. The speaker mentioned research on why more U.S. females go to college than males. Joyce enthusiastically realized, "Lo and behold, he almost had the exact same explanation as our young tribal leader! It was a humbling reminder that if you want the truth, listen to the children."

The Ultimate Goal: Leaving a Legacy of Good

His ice-blue eyes were as piercing as ever, but his hands and mouth quivered uncontrolled as he tried to speak. I was visiting one of my most important mentors, who was suffering from a progressive form of Parkinson's disease. He was connected to several different tubes, including oxygen, and I could tell he was frustrated when he struggled to talk. It was painful to see this man who had given me so much enduring such a merciless hardship and nearing the end of his journey.

Andy Alexander is a good friend and classmate of mine from the U.S. Air Force Academy and his family have played important roles in my life. His mom, Judy, was my real estate agent when I bought my first house and when I started my business, Native Discovery, his dad, Glynn, had become my accountant and so much more.

Glynn had an easygoing demeanor and a Texas drawl that always seemed to calm me when I was crawling out of my skin from the stress of starting and running my own business. He was a skilled and experienced CPA, and his guidance was golden on the ins and outs of business structure, tax payments and reporting, payroll, and the multitude of details that are involved in running a successful business. But the coaching, the empathetic conversations, and his wisdom, encouragement, and generosity of spirit were truly priceless to me. There were times when I truly didn't know if I could make this new endeavor work and each time I went to his office to ask about another confusing detail or vent about another stressful issue, the scene was always the same. I'd walk in and he'd lean back in his chair, hands clasped behind his head and sporting a wide-as-Texas smile. His eyes were ice-blue, but they radiated warmth. He'd brightly ask, "How's it going, D.J.?" and I'd immediately relax, knowing he already had the answers—and my back—every time.

In their living room, Judy smiled and doted on Glynn, but I could feel the tension of worry and fear in them both. I leaned forward and held Glynn's hand and told him how much he'd meant to me, how dear of a friend and mentor he'd been, how I wouldn't have made it without him. I told him how much of a deep, positive, and lasting impact he'd had on my life, my family, and those I serve. I've rarely had a more powerful connection than I did in that moment, honoring an elder who'd meant so much to me and saying thank you for his influence and impact in my life. His mouth trembled and his eyes filled with tears and mine did too. Even writing this now, I feel a swell of emotion rise inside of me. Glynn passed away a few months later, with his family beside him.

Every day of our lives, we are leaving a legacy with our service to others. That legacy is most brightly displayed through the people we impact, the lives we touch, and the way we share our gifts of time, talent, and wisdom. The heart of the warrior role is service to others, and we can do that throughout our lifetimes, coaching or mentoring others not just in our working years but also as we get older and are able to share distilled knowledge and experience, also known as wisdom. At the end of your days, who in your tribe will be grateful for your influence, time, and contribution of your knowledge, wisdom, and encouragement? It's a question that can guide us to purposefully contribute each day of our lives.

CONCLUSION

'm writing these words as an act of defiance, facing my own fears of opening up about where I am and how I got here, in the hopes that it may give you encouragement to face your own "stuff" to move ahead in a stronger, healthier way in your life. And I honestly cannot think of a better, more genuine way to conclude this book or else I would offer that instead. So here it goes . . .

For over two decades, I've worked hard to be a reliable resource of positivity, encouragement, and strength for the clients I served, and built a successful business because of it. It was so much easier to focus on serving others well than it was to take care of myself by dealing with my own past and painful issues.

When the pandemic hit, my packed calendar of booked events in 2020 evaporated in a span of three days in late March. My family relied on me and my reaction to this suddenly blank calendar was visceral. I felt like I'd been punched in the gut. I immediately started getting up to speed on virtual delivery (which I'd never done before) and dusted off a never-used Microsoft LifeCam that was shoved into the back of an office drawer. In the following weeks, I started slowly rebuilding and getting back on track.

Then I got news that rocked me to my core. My wife said she wanted a separation. I was devastated. It felt like the bottom floor of my life fell away and I was in freefall.

The next thing I knew, I was sitting alone, isolated as the pandemic raged, in a dimly lit rental unit, crying my eyes out on a stranger's couch, wondering why the hell this was happening to me. But I knew why. Kind of. There is a line from my first book, *The Tiny Warrior*, that reads: *However long or far you go, you cannot outrun your life's problems when those problems are within.* That line haunted me from the moment I wrote it so many years ago. I had been running my ass off to keep distance between myself and painful issues from my past. Even in my second book, *Spirit on the Run*, the main character, Derek, and his battle with unresolved issues is more like me than I'd like to admit. Now the running was over, and the problems were front and center. My warrior within was being called out to respond, even in my brokenness.

The first month of separation was like living a nightmare of shock, heartbreak, loneliness, and days and nights shrouded in a shame fog. I'd never felt like such a failure. When I was at my lowest, I thought about my daughters. They would also be witness to how I handled this adversity. What kind of example would I want to show them? When I finally pushed through that initial period, I began eagerly pouring myself into the healing work I had needed to do my whole life. I started to lean heavily on principles that I'd been using and teaching for many years and saw them all with new eyes. Reminding myself of my values and what I valued, using my medicine to heal and making self-care a priority, facing my fears head-on, reaching out to other warriors for support, embracing humility and growth, navigating change and setbacks, creating a solid environment, and taking consistent, focused action all played a vital role in my progress. And during the hardest moments, remembering to keep putting one foot in front of the other was *absolutely priceless*. I can tell you with unwavering confidence, these principles were tested in the crucible of struggle, moment by moment—and they happen to be the very principles that are densely sown throughout the entire book you just read.

Though this has been the most painful chapter of my life, it also been the most transformative. I've never experienced growth this profound, or so rapidly, or been able to see things with such clarity. But I've never experienced this depth of darkness or isolation either. We can't see the stars in daylight. I felt like I've been in ceremony for the last two years and the bounty of lessons learned through this agonizing transition have not gone unnoticed—or uncollected. Like a shoot breaking the hull of a seed and flowering up through cracked concrete, we sometimes must first be broken to experience new growth.

I also learned we sometimes must go backward to start moving forward again. As I learned to finally understand my past, what happened, and how I got here, I began healing and leaned forward into my work. What I found was a subtle shift that made a world of difference. So many of the groups I worked with were suffering the ravages of the pandemic: elevated stress, isolation, feelings of loss, depletion, and a struggle to stay focused or prioritize self-care. What I had been going through provided novel insight. I've always viewed my work as "providing for the providers" but now was doing it at a more meaningful and empathetic level than ever before. I could hear differently, respond differently. I was connecting in a different way, and I was serving better because of it.

That spark reminded me of what led me to my work, and I reengaged with a renewed passion. I knew, more than ever, that I was made for the work I'm blessed to do. I resumed talks with PBS that led to becoming the writer, producer, and host of my own TV special, *Discovering Your Warrior Spirit.* I worked for months on a book proposal and got a fantastic new literary agent and a dream contract with Penguin Random House for this book. Things were feeling and looking better than ever, and everything finally seemed to be emerging from the fires.

Of course, life is always challenging. And sometimes when things already suck, they can suck even more. While writing this book, I got rear-ended in a car accident and suffered sharp tingling and frequent numbness in both arms and my right hand from damage done to my neck. There were days I couldn't write, frustrated to tears as I made more mistakes than accurate hits on the keyboard. And in the end, after over a year of separation, the reconciliation I'd hoped for wasn't to be. My wife and I decided to divorce. Sometimes we don't get do-overs. But through it all, I've determined to take what I've learned and use it to be a better dad to my daughters and a better partner in my future relationships.

At the beginning of my separation, I was resistant to reach out for support, feeling overwhelmed with shame, guilt, and a feeling of failure. I was afraid of judgment and criticism, already feeling a full-volume assault from within. And I was acting like my own worst enemy by isolating. Then I was reminded that "warriors never fight alone" and started reaching out for support, getting out of my own way. Even in my work, I felt more than ever like an impostor. I thought, "Who am I to talk about resiliency, courage, fighting through challenges, healing, and strength in service?" I was struggling to even get out of bed in the beginning. But after the last few years, I think, "Who am I *not* to share these things?" Now it feels mandatory. I don't feel like an impostor anymore, but more like a guinea pig in my own lab, retesting hypotheses, reproving theories, and reconfirming good results in my own worst circumstances.

This whole experience has reiterated to me why these principles matter—and why they work. I've been teaching these ideas for many years and use them constantly but had no idea just how valuable they would be for me when I needed them most. Though we all have our own unique struggles, I share all of what I have in this conclusion in the spirit of vulnerability, in hopes that someone reading this may not feel alone as they battle their own storms. These principles served me well and I feel poised to serve at a higher level than ever before. This whole experience was a reminder that through it all we can endure even when things fall apart, defying the gravity of those moments. We *can* still own our power to serve well, fight for and protect what we believe in, heal ourselves—and deliver when it matters.

I'm still standing. I'm still in the fight.

Stay strong on *your* warrior path.

—D.J. Vanas

ACKNOWLEDGMENTS

Like a stone chipped into an arrowhead, we can be shaped and sharpened through the years by the people and experiences we encounter. I've been so fortunate to have more wonderful people and experiences than I can count. I'm who I am because of them. I'd also like to say chi-miigwech (thank you very much) to all those who have supported, encouraged, and believed in me and my message through the years. I'm where I am because of you.

Any great undertaking benefits from great support and this book effort was no exception. I'm so thankful for those who contributed to add horsepower to this message, the ones who cheered me on during this process, and the ones who have done it for many decades now. From the bottom of my heart, thank you to the following contributors for your insight, your vulnerability, and sharing your inspiring stories: LeAnn Thieman, Nancy Griffin, Karen Goodnight, Julie Garreau, Juanita Mullen, Phyllis Kalifeh, Katherine Campbell, Martha Kerr, John Herrington, Kevin Basik, Shane Coyne, Herb Clah Jr., Robyn Sunday-Allen, Joyce McFarland, Alex

White, Sonya Tetnowski, Allison Wise, Jonathan Baines, and Holly Figueroa.

Those whose ideas I shared or who got roped into the stories I told, which include Aaron Lawson, Troy Harting, Mark LeBlanc, Mike Pine, Ruben Gonzalez, Donnell Smith, Andy Alexander and his parents Judy and Glynn, Doug Ericksen, and Coach Ed Weichers. You have my admiration and gratitude.

Adrianne Maddux, Dina Romero, Danny Garceau, Terry Ashby, Anton Treuer, and Doreen Williams for the supportive and insightful conversations.

The countless elders across Indian Country and First Nations communities who have guided my life and my work, and to all our tribal nations; your resiliency, strength, and beauty continues to inspire. To my ceremonial family, your patience, wisdom, and examples illuminated the path I'm still on today.

The incredible team at Penguin Random House: Stefanie Rosenblum Brody in publicity, Heather Faulls in marketing, Deb Lewis in sales, and my superstar editor Nina Rodriguez-Marty—you have been a guide, a coach, a trusted teammate, and a cheerleader all at once (you made me believe I could actually do this!). And thank you to Niki Papadopoulos for believing in me and offering this amazing opportunity.

My wonderful agent, Carol Mann, for your encouragement, business savvy, expert guidance, and belief in me and my ability to share my message with a bigger world.

The United States Air Force Academy and the United States Air Force, for shaping my life, providing opportunities to serve well and to recognize and grow my capabilities, strengthen my character, courage, and confidence, to see the world, and form bonds with the best friends I'll ever know.

Dianna Booher, not sure whether to call her the book sherpa or book cook, but she has a huge heart and an amazing ability to guide people to craft their ideas into a potent plan for a manuscript. I'm so grateful for her coaching.

To my people, my tribe, the ones who stood by me and served as my own personal cheering section:

My daughter Gabrielle, from the moment you were born, you've amazed me. When my clumsy hands first touched you to help deliver you into the world, I didn't realize you were delivering me into a whole new world too. You inspire me with your hilarious antics, exuberant spirit, intuitive heart, and analytical mind and a character that has always focused on justice and empathy for others. You're courageous in your life and have challenged me to be a better person. I love you always and forever.

My daughter Isabella, you were born with a warrior spirit, fighting thirty-nine days in the NICU to be here so you could share the splendor and magic of who you are with the world. You're an old soul with deep wisdom, a brilliant mind, and a beautiful spirit. You walk your path with a great sense of curiosity, humor, and always surprise me with your insights and inspire me with your resiliency, grit, and strength—and I know it all protects a tender heart. I'm honored to be your dad. I love you always and forever.

Kimberly Buchanan, my beautiful and artistic little sister, for her love, laughter, support, and holding my hand and my heart throughout my life. I'm so blessed to be your brother and thank you for your patience, understanding, and forgiving me for sticking a roly-poly in your nose when you were in diapers. And to my brother-in-law, Wes, for your kindness, support . . . and our therapeutic video-game sessions.

Aaron Lawson for decades of friendship, support, and adventures. Can't believe we survived the Kalalau Trail . . . wait, that was your #$@%ing idea! Never again, but I love you, man.

The Harting Family—Troy, Dana, and my goddaughter Allie—for your decades of love, friendship, support, and always providing sanctuary during the stormy times (as long as I'm cheering for the Steelers). Troy, you're brilliant, disciplined, and hilarious, all wrapped up in a taco shell of fierce loyalty as a friend. Mmmm . . . tacos.

Tom Dawson—we've been friends since we were teenagers, but in these last few years, you have been a sage, guide, coach, and the best of friends during one of the hardest times in my life. And thank you for helping to calm my nerves before flying out to do the filming for my PBS special, saying, "Don't be nervous, one step at time. There's no guarantee you're even going to get there." Now that's perspective.

To my TOU crew (Those of Us) Arthur Schwartz, Dave Keller, Shane Coyne, Jon Heller, and the Godfather of it all,

Kevin Basik. Your encouragement gave me strength. Kevin is one of the funniest, most energetic, and positive people I know. You're a transmitter of goodness, my friend, keep that signal strong.

Dixie Dorman for your wisdom, courage, and example of resiliency. You're a fierce and wonderful mom to Lilly and Brooke, a dedicated educator, and, yes, a nerdy gangsta. I'm proud to be your friend.

Joe Atkins and Iris Rosario-Atkins for your support and love. You cradled my heart with warm hands when I needed it most. And Iris, you may have retired from fifty years of nursing, but you're still a caregiver of souls and still helping others heal.

Thomas and Ally Wise for creating a safe harbor of kindness, care, and encouragement throughout this project and a place to laugh, heal, and enjoy the best popcorn on the planet, made by Thomas. And to Omar Quintero for your artistic gifts and sharing them with so many others, including me.

Authors who strengthened and inspired me through the last couple years—David Goggins, Brené Brown, Angeline Boulley, Matthew McConaughey, Ryan Holiday, Thich Nat Hahn, Tony Robbins, Viktor Frankl, Penache Desai, Pema Chodron, Kevin Hart, Simon Sinek, Richard Wagamese, Alice Miller, Richard Rohr, Carol Dweck, Julia Cameron, Pia Mellody, Edith Eger, Yung Pueblo, and Kamal Ravikant.

And, finally, to all the people who have dedicated their lives to serving others well, even in the face of the recent chaos, not for the recognition or compensation. But because you're driven to contribute, make the world a better place, and leave a legacy of good in your wake—and because you feel it's in you to do so. You continue to inspire me and my work. You are warriors all.

Index